For Mary Doxey,
    In appreciation for your
support and friendship
through the years.
        Elise Winter
            1982

Dinner at the Mansion

To
the memory of
my mother
Mamie Veazey Varner
1890-1982

Dinner
at
the Mansion

by

Elise Winter

with Frank E. Smith

YOKNAPATAWPHA PRESS
Oxford, Mississippi

All royalties from the sale of this book will
be contributed to the Mississippi Children's
Mental Health Foundation.

Published by Yoknapatawpha Press, Inc.
P.O. Box 248, Oxford, MS 38655

ISBN 0-916242-21-8   LC 82-60326

Book design by Gary Hauser

Printed in the United States of America

Contents

Acknowledgment

I read some where a long time ago that one must have a child, plant a tree and write a book to be truly fulfilled. With three marvelous daughters and many years of planting occasional trees, somehow I never planned to write a book. But then, politics does place one in strange circumstances.

When William Winter and I married I never thought or even wildly suspected that politics would play a part in my life. Young love is foolish, for he was even then a freshman member of the Mississippi Legislature. Indeed, politics, has been a leading force in our lives together and he, the consummate politician, has had a tremendous influence on my life—even to the point of writing a book. Because of his urging, I have kept a journal during our time here in the Mansion. After a few days of this I grew very discouraged, feeling that I was certainly less than articulate and that each day was filled to capacity without having this additional task thrust upon me. With his constant urging and his strong encouragement I continued, thinking that maybe my journal might some day jog his memory and help him, the writer and historian that he is, write *his* book.

But until that time and with the very able assistance of Frank Smith, I have attempted to record some of the special events that have taken place here at the Governor's Mansion during the administration of my very favorite Governor, William Winter. This would not have been possible without Frank Smith, who has a way of putting into nice words and acceptable phrases some of my own thoughts and halting expressions. I am indeed grateful.

And then how do you say thank you to my fellow workers in the office who work each day to make the

Winter administration responsive to the people, concerned and caring, dignified and professional. For all these friends, and especially Mary Al Alford (who typed it all), Virginia Parsons, Tommie and Melba Darras, Janice Ammann, Kitty Czarnieki, Dorothy Milton and Dusty Perkins, thank you is too small but is written with love and respect.

E.W.
May 21, 1982
Jackson, Mississippi

FOREWORD
by
Willie Morris

When I was editing *Harper's Magazine* in New York, I read a brief wire service story on a back page of *The New York Times* about a federal court order out of New Orleans that certain key areas in the Deep South—especially my beloved Mississippi—must massively integrate the public schools in January, 1970, after the Christmas vacation. This was sixteen years after the watershed U.S. Supreme Court decision of 1954. I resolved from an office on Park Avenue that I must come home and write about Mississippi in its most poignant and challenging moment of change.

In the course of my work I had lunch in the Patio Club in Jackson with Elise and William Winter. At that time Winter was not holding public office. Although I had never met them before, I had naturally heard much about them—about their grace, civility, and courage in our state, and in America. I still have my notes on that luncheon in a cardboard box somewhere on Faculty Row at Ole Miss. But what I remember most indelibly was the beauty and commitment of Elise Winter to the finest aspects of Mississippi, and indeed the candor and forcefulness of her distinguished consort. More specifically, with Mrs. Winter, I sensed—long before the national flowering of what is now known as Women's Liberation—a woman who by her imagination and intelligence would someday, if not then, make all Mississippians proud.

I am deeply taken by *Dinner at the Mansion*, by its quiet feeling of drama, by the warmth and clear-headedness of the lovely woman who, in 1982, is so perceptive of the splendid old house on Capitol Street over which she presides, not to mention the promise of our native ground.

Ten years later, I came home to Mississippi from Long Island to be a writer-in-residence at the University of Mississippi. Our state is likely the most *communal* of all the fifty states, and so it was no great surprise to me when my telephone rang one Sunday afternoon to find that it was the Governor dialing me himself.

William Winter had recently been inaugurated. On that Sunday he wanted to welcome me home where he said I belonged. Then he said: "I hear Plimpton and Styron are coming to see you."

He was referring, of course, to my friends the writers, George Plimpton and William Styron. I confirmed that Plimpton was arriving on a quick visit to Ole Miss in two weeks and that Styron would be here shortly after that. Being a man of fine humor, the Governor agreed to a plan I suggested. Since Plimpton's great-grandfather was Adelbert P. Ames, the Radical Reconstructionist Governor of Mississippi after the Civil War against whom impeachment papers were eventually brought, Governor Winter would issue a pardon to Ames and grant Plimpton a twelve-hour safe conduct through Mississippi. His pardon, however, would not include George's other great-grandfather, Benjamin Butler of Massachusetts, the occupying general of New Orleans, better known in the South as "Beast," so reviled in those days that the citizens of New Orleans later manufactured "Beast Butler Chamber Pots" with the likeness of Plimpton's great-grandfather on the bottom.

At Ole Miss an overflow audience came to hear The Plimp. As part of my introduction I read the letter to him from the Governor:

Dear Mr. Plimpton:

". . . You are an honored guest today at our State University. Your literary and editorial genius is notable. Your athletic talent has encouraged you to play quarterback, throw baseballs, drive racing cars, box against champions, and slam cymbals together in the symphony orchestra. Your comradeship with our Southern writers in New York City, where you so graciously keep them out of trouble, has helped bring the "Grand Ole Union" back together again.

As Governor of Mississippi, I herewith extend a pardon to your great-grandfather, Adelbert P. Ames, the Republican Reconstructionist Governor of our beloved State, and present a document of safe conduct through the ghosts of old enemy lines. I pledge that you shall remain free and unmolested in the Sovereign State of Mississippi for 12 hours, beginning at 9:45 a.m. today, February 26, 1980, ending at 9:45 p.m. on that day, when I understand that your plane departs north from Memphis. I cannot, however, speak for the Governor of Tennessee on this matter.
With all best wishes from the people of Mississippi, I am

Sincerely yours,
William F. Winter
Governor

Plimpton was so relieved by this pardon of at least one of his great-grandfathers, as well as by his temporary safe conduct, that he gave a classic, virtuoso performance at Ole Miss that day.

As for Styron, the Governor during our telephone conversation invited him and his wife Rose, my son David—then a student at Hampshire College, Amherst—and myself to stay as guests in the Governor's Mansion in Jackson. He and I also thought it would be a good idea to have a three-man panel, the Governor and Styron and I, before an appropriate audience to discuss the Southern past and present.

William Winter is a thoughtful student of history and literature. Although I was not aware of it at the time, his invitation to Bill Styron and me was part of a historic plan, without precedent in previous administrations, to bring to the Mansion writers, artists, diplomats and industrialists for a cultural exchange which would expose Mississippians to the best minds and talents of America and also allow the guests to take with them a sense of the best that Mississippi has to offer—its people and its traditions. With the help of the beautiful and gifted Elise, Governor Winter has made this Mansion guest program a memorable event that must certainly become incumbent on our future Governors.

Much was brought to fruition in 1980 in the election of

William Winter as Governor. For years he had been the focus for those thousands of Mississippians who represented, in Lincoln's words, "the better angels of our nature"—he stood for racial moderation in the 1950s and 1960s when it was unpopular and even dangerous to do so—and his victory was a cause for reaffirmation among those who had remained steadfast for the civilizing values in the difficult years.

As Governor, William Winter set about marshaling the resources of his state, not the least of which is the remarkable literary tradition of Mississippi. Well into the late Twentieth Century, Mississippi has retained much of its communal origins, and along with that a sense of continuity, of the enduring past and the flow of the generations—an awareness, if you will, of human history. William Faulkner, the poet and chronicler of Mississippi, understood how deeply we care for it despite what it was and is—the gulf between its manners and morals, the extraordinary apposition of its violence and kindliness. There is something that matters in a state which elicits in its sons and daughters of both races, wherever they live, such emotions of fidelity and rage and passion. "Time is very important to us because it has dealt with us," Eudora Welty says. "We have suffered and learned and progressed through it."

Bill Styron had only been to Mississippi once, and that was the briefest of visits. He came down one oppressively hot July day in 1962 for Faulkner's funeral in Oxford, on assignment from *Life Magazine.* This time Bill's trip to Mississippi would be a happier one. He came to Oxford to address the Ole Miss students. Like many artists who are involved with the sadness of the human adventure, my comrade Styron appreciates the possibilities of wit, and he had his Ole Miss audience poised between tears and laughter which, given the circumstances of things, is not a bad condition to be in at all. A few days later we met Rose at the airport in Jackson and made our way to the Governor's Mansion.

Jackson, like Washington, D.C., before it, was a planned city, and lies near the geographical center of the state. Thomas Jefferson himself, though having never been here, provided some of the earliest plans for its streets and parks. The city of my birth and of my childhood visits to my grandparents on North Jefferson has undergone two distinct destructions. The first came at Sherman's hand in 1863, months before the burning of Atlanta and the March to the Sea. After his and Grant's successful landing on the east bank of the Mississippi south of Vicksburg, he moved toward Jackson to destroy the railroad junction and make the city useless for General Joseph E. Johnston. His job was so thorough that for years afterward Jackson was known as "Chimneyville." The State Capitol and the Governor's Mansion were among the few substantial structures he chose to spare.

The second destruction came from ostensibly friendly hands, in the form of the New South of recent years. The lovely and somnolent little city of my boyhood is no more—whole neighborhoods and whole city blocks ripped raw, and the emergence of the giant shopping malls and suburbias. There are things here now which my grandfather, who was born shortly after the Civil War and who died in 1953, would find unfathomable. If he stepped out of his grave in the old section of the Raymond cemetery and came back to Jackson, I suspect the scene along Interstate 55 with its mile upon mile of franchise establishments would astonish and frighten him. Modern-day Capitol Street and the Metrocenter Mall would leave him mystified, as would the traffic snarls and giant complexes and insurance chains along the quiet streets where we rode the Number Four bus. Remembering Jackson as it once was, I am left only with a broken heart.

But here, suddenly, on Capitol Street, the Governor's

Mansion loomed before us, a cherished and familiar place amidst the dwindling of dreams. As Rose and Bill and David and I sighted it from our car in a soft dusk of springtime, it had a touch of lost moments for me when I walked barefoot on the sidewalk and looked upward toward its curtained windows and wondered what monumental events might be transpiring in there. We stopped in our car for a moment to absorb its antebellum Greek Revival dignity, the gazebos and fountains and gardens outside and the oaks my Uncle Henry Foote's wife planted there, and the semi-circular front portico with its four Corinthian columns and delicate capitals which so resemble the south portico of the White House. The Mansion itself is not as large or imposing as the White House, but possesses a grace all its own, the grace of character gained through suffering and loss.

At the portico we were greeted by several servants in white jackets (I later learned they were trusties from Parchman, the state penal farm) and waiting for us inside the door were the Governor, Elise, their two daughters, and the ebullient Charlotte Capers of the state archives. It was a fine Southern welcome, followed by a tour of the grand parlors and foyers of the main floor, all dominated by a magnificent curved staircase. This Mansion is, in fact, the second oldest official executive residence in continuous use in the country behind the White House.

I remembered the description I recently had read by a gentleman from Natchez to this small frontier town in the 1840s: "Much is anticipated by the elite here. When the Executive Mansion shall be ready, levees, re-unions, routs, conversations, dejeuners, and soirees will be the order of the day, and our political metropolis will become more gay, fashionable, and attractive. I have serious ideas of moving thither."

Our hosts escorted us upstairs to our rooms, then left us to get ready for dinner. William Winter is a tall, slender man of 59 who talks and listens with an intensity that is by no means grave, and there is, God bless him, a touch of mischief in his gentle patrician chemistry, as when he assigned Rose and Bill Styron the Bilbo Bedroom.

The four of us wandered these splendid rooms in the spirit of children freshly awakened on Christmas morning. We felt adventurous on this night. David showed us his hand-carved four-poster bed in a pineapple design and the view from his room of a lush green garden. Rose Styron, whose legendary Baltimore beauty has always been in full flush at such moments (she was remarkably beautiful on a midnight visit we once made to Appomattox, and her husband says she was equally radiant at the Parthenon) pointed out the Boston looking glass and the red antique fabric and the gas chandeliers and the etagere between the windows. I took them into my enormous room and told them, as I had been advised, that Sherman had slept here after the fall of Vicksburg, not to mention the fabulous Mississippian Leontyne Price when she was a guest during the Winters' Inaugural.

"Wait til I tell my friends in New York!" Styron interrupted. I noticed he had been ruminating. "Sleeping on Bilbo's bed! Come on in here." He tried the mattress on the tester bed, then stood back to take it all in. As with most Southern boys of a certain generation, Styron was not unacquainted with the follies and complexities of Theodore G. Bilbo, and indeed had written of him at length in his majestic novel *Sophie's Choice*.

As I lay in my bed (and Sherman's, and Leontyne Price's) before sleep came that night, listening to the rain falling steadily on the new Chimneyville, and the thunder rumbling in from the Delta, and the gentle nocturnal echoes of the Capitol Street of my childhood, I dwelled upon the arguments that must have taken place under this ancient roof on national allegiance and sectional interest before that long-ago war, of the strains of music and the laughter of the Mississippi belles lost now to dust, of Bilbo walking the room across the foyer in the witching hours.

Quite early the next morning I was awakened by a rude shaking. It was Bill Styron. "Get up!" he said. "I've got something to tell you." At first I thought the Mansion might be on fire, such was the look in his eye. "I had the most extraordinary dream," he said. "I'm sure it's because I was sleeping in Bilbo's bed. Listen to this —." He had an appointment with Henry Kissinger, it was hazy whether he was supposed to meet Kissinger in Washington or New York, but it was on some question of overwhelming national importance, and Kissinger had to see him. "It was the strangest dream I ever had. All that damned Bilbo's doing," Styron complained. He kept talking about it in the tour we made in one of the Mansion's cars that day of Raymond, Port Gibson, and Vicksburg.

That evening a capacity crowd came to the "William and Bill and Willie Show" in the auditorium at Millsaps, which Hodding Carter at the height of the racial crisis called "the most courageous little college in America." The topic was to reflect on our region as a great source and training ground for writers, and to discuss something of the Southern past in the burdens of its history and in the changes now taking place.

Without intending to, the Governor stole the show. He began by introducing several dozen of my friends and neighbors from my native Yazoo City whom he had invited to the discussion and to a reception later at the Mansion. It was easy that evening to see why the quality of leadership he was bringing to the state was different from anything Mississippians have gotten from any of their Governors in modern history. He is articulate and scholarly, yet he has not spurned the colorful rhetoric of his political tradition. He spoke of Mississippi's writers as the finest part of the heritage of the state, of the communal and historical sense which has contributed to this heritage. He discussed literature in relation to social changes, of the old grievances in the racial climate and the possibilities residing in the new awareness. I do not have notes on that session, but I did write on a scrap of paper which I have before me now: "He is saying things which no Governor of a Deep Southern state has ever said, and with the eloquence of a Stevenson or a John Kennedy. This is a historic moment for Mississippi."

On the way back to the Mansion, the Governor and Styron and I were talking. Writers have terrible things to get over, Bill said—such as destructive reviews when they are getting started. For a politician the equivalent has to be *defeat.* The Governor remembered, he said, his first loss for the governorship. "I never wanted anything more badly. I thought I had it won, that I deserved it. I thought it was the worst thing that could ever happen to me. I didn't want to face myself or anyone else for a long time." We entered the gates of the Mansion, floodlit now against the threatening sky. "Then it dawned on me—you have to keep going. Not feel sorry for yourself, but *keep on going.*"

On this and subsequent visits to the Mansion, I was glad to be a guest of Elise and William Winter. I will not forget the toast the Governor solicited from Leontyne Price at a dinner in her honor in 1981: "God Bless America" sung *a capella* which majestically reverberated across the chandeliers and through the old house. I remember, too, the evening for Walker Percy, when my friends Mr. Percy and Eudora Welty were absorbed next to me at the dinner table in an intense, whispered conversation. What were these literary masters discussing? The Romantic Poets? The Nineteenth Century Russian novelists? Onomatopoeia? How to explain their serious countenances? As a fellow writer I, of course, eavesdropped. Mr. Percy was explaining to Miss Welty in much detail the plot of the television series of our day, *The Incredible Hulk.*

Elise Winter's book gives us an insight into such matters,

and into our state. It is, in its own quiet way, a self-revealing book, for what it reveals finally is the most hard-earned quality of any individual, or any society. That quality, we pray, is civilization.

Introduction

BEFORE WE moved into the Governor's Mansion, on Sunday night, January 20, 1980, two days before the inauguration on January 22, my ideas about the lovely old house were really very hazy—I thought of receptions and dinners and glamorous social events, but with little understanding of the intricate preparations involved, and the painstaking execution of the plans.

From the time of our arrival I have had little chance to think about the Mansion as a glamorous place—I've been too busy with the day-to-day process of running a house and tending to a household. It will always be an interesting place, but the glamour began to fade when I realized that there were household problems here just as at my own home.

The similarities between our house and this house include the fact that the roof leaks here, too, and the washing machine and the dryers die their own deaths from time to time.

There was the night during our first spring when the freezing mechanism in the huge walk-in food locker in the basement went "on the blink." I called a friend who could take the frozen food into his warehouse, and we were just getting it unloaded when someone asked, "Do you realize that it is flooding in the basement?"

Our good neighbors at the First Baptist Church saved us from that catastrophe, for they loaned us their suction vacuum which kept the water out enough to hold down the damage until the rain ceased the next morning.

1

To complicate matters further, the same heavy rains caused a leak in the Bilbo room. It was necessary to put buckets there to catch the drips. Later when the plaster fell I very calmly thought, "Of course, and what else?" I guess a house is just made of bricks and mortar and subject to that sort of thing no matter who slept in it or how old or historic it may be!

Not long after we had been here, the staff from the Department of Archives and History, which has the responsibility for preserving the Mansion as an historic landmark, told me that the historic areas open for visits by the general public—the four bedrooms upstairs and three parlors and dining room downstairs—were in need of repainting.

This was really my first experience with government regulations but for work on a state property, the project must be advertised for bidding. There must be at least three bids and it is necessary to accept the low bid or be prepared to do a lot of explaining. When the bids were opened for this work, I was utterly amazed for the high bid was $25,000, the next $23,000 and the low bid was $6,800. I was not prepared for the high cost or the wide variance. I even wondered if the low bidder knew how to paint at all. William and I are very conscious of our responsibility to keep the costs of government to a minimum to the state but I could not help thinking that if the low bid were a little higher or closer to the other bids I would have understood it better. Nevertheless the low bidder began his work and I almost stood on his ladder to be sure that he could indeed paint.

We had estimated that it would take a month or six weeks to do the job, but Mr. Cheatham's crew did it in eight days, working right through the weekend, and with a minimum of disruption to the Mansion. Mr. Cheatham belied his name, and the work he performed was thoroughly satisfactory.

Moving into the routine of the day-to-day operation of the Mansion has made the glamour fade, but it has also made me a serious student of the history of this lovely old dwelling, and the use that can be made of it in improving the quality of government and the quality of life in our state.

Jackson, the capital city of Mississippi, did not begin to become the metropolis of Mississippi until after 1900. Jackson had its beginning when it was literally picked out of the wilderness to become the capital. Doak's Stand, a tavern stop along the Natchez Trace, was the inhabited point near the site selected, which was chosen by a legislative commission seeking a location nearer the geographic center of the new state than Natchez, the first capital.

The new town was named Jackson, in honor of Andrew Jackson, the most popular hero of the day, even before he became President. General Jackson had many Mississippi friends and connections, in a relationship that began before statehood and before the Battle of New Orleans.

The growing pains of town to city began to show symptoms after 1900. Capitol Street, moving broadly west from the handsome state capitol building, was the center of commercial activity in Jackson as most state government shifted to the New Capitol two blocks north of the Mansion. Front footage on the street began to be identified as of great value commercially, and real estate developers noted the attractions of the block which was utilized by only one building—the Governor's Mansion.

The word had spread that the Mansion had physically deteriorated in the seventy years that it had housed the various Governors of Mississippi, and that before long the state was going to have to spend a lot of money to repair the structure. Why not open the way for more commercial development on Capitol Street by tearing down the old

3

Mansion, selling the block to a real estate developer, using the money to build a new house for the governor outside the "high value" district, and probably have a substantial sum left over for the state treasury?

The scheme had attractions, and it was presented to the State Legislature with formidable backing in 1908.

The actual disclosure of the plan brought a quick reaction. Organized opposition was politely but firmly displayed by many civic groups, foremost of which were the ladies patriotic organizations, of which Jackson boasted at least half a dozen. They had cooperative help from their sister organizations in the other cities and towns of the state.

"Will Mississippi destroy what Sherman would not burn?" became a cry of proud Mississippians from Holly Springs to Biloxi, with voteless women in the forefront of the protests. The Legislature heeded their cries, and the Governor's Mansion was saved for Mississippians of future generations.

The Mississippi Legislature, in 1833, had authorized the construction of a "suitable house for the governor, in the town of Jackson," and appropriated $10,000.00 for the purpose. At the time Jackson was little more than a hamlet, and the "house" designated for construction by the Legislature would obviously be entitled to be properly called a "mansion."

A permanent state capitol was also authorized at this same time, and the construction of the two important new buildings for Mississippi was entrusted to a new state architect. William Nichols, a native of Bath, England, came to Mississippi after sojourns in North Carolina and Louisiana, and was chosen as architect in competition with a number of other talented young men who had come south as a result of the fabled "flush times" of our early statehood.

In addition to the Old Capitol and the Mansion,

4

Nichols' best known additional work in Mississippi is the legendary Lyceum Building on the campus of the University of Mississippi. Nichols is believed to have designed a number of private residences in the state, but identification has never been complete. He eventually made his home in Lexington, MIssissippi where he is buried.

The new statehouse, which we now know as the Old Capitol, had first priority with Nichols, but the Governor's house which he completed in 1842, had the same classic Greek Revival strength and beauty. Nichols proposed to "avoid a profusion of ornament, and to adhere to a plain republican simplicity, as comporting with the dignity of the state." The building met that standard, but its two stories and basement, fronted by a portico with the classic Corinthian columns, was also far and away the most commanding residence in Jackson, and it quickly became identified as the "Governor's Mansion."

Governor Tilghman M. Tucker moved in with his family in 1842, and became the first Governor in residence. Today the Mansion is the second oldest executive residence in the United States continuously occupied by state governors. Only the Virginia Mansion, on the grounds of the capitol in Richmond, has been in longer use.

The main floor of the Mansion is entered through an octagonal vestibule. To the left, or west, is a large drawing room. On the other side, to the east, is a dining room which can be enlarged with the opening of folding doors. A grand staircase begins in the central hall, leading to four spacious bedchambers on the second floor. The first governors to occupy the mansion used the second floor bedchambers for their own families, but in later days extension of the building to the north has provided the actual living quarters for the Governors.

As the center of state government and of a rich agricultural area, Jackson grew rapidly during the years before the Civil War, but it did not become the center of wealth typified by towns like Natchez and Vicksburg on the Mississippi River, and Holly Springs and Columbus, trade centers for the rich plantation areas of the north and prairie regions of the state.

Consequently few private ante bellum mansions of the type that are still today the glory of the river cities were built in Jackson. The Governor's Mansion was identified and accepted as the finest residence in Jackson. Because the Mansion symbolized the fierce resistance to invading federal troops in 1862 and 1863, General William T. Sherman chose the Mansion for a Union victory dinner after the fall of Jackson on July 17, 1863.

Union troops occupied Jackson four times during the period of the Vicksburg campaign and other active fighting in Mississippi, and Jackson suffered greatly in physical damage. Sherman's troops put the town to the torch, and much of the town was literally burned to the ground. The mansion was one of the few residences intact in a town some called "Chimneyville."

The spacious, isolated grounds of the mansion may have been one reason it escaped damage from fire—another may have been that the Union officers were foreseeing use for the mansion like the victory dinner. At any rate the Governor's Mansion survived, and came to be regarded as a symbol of the strength and surviving power of the state during the hard times of reconstruction and the post-war struggle against poverty that characterized life in Mississippi for the quarter of a century following the war.

For many Mississippians, the stately Mansion became a symbol of the quality of life to which they aspired on behalf of their state.

Through the years, the Governor's Mansion has had to undergo several reconditioning and rehabilitation programs, but it is still actively functioning as a center of Mississippi government and official life. Thanks to the genius of William Nichols, the foresight of the Mississippi

Legislature, the forbearance of General Sherman, and the loving care and generosity of many first families, the Governor's Mansion deserves its recognition as a National Historic Landmark.

Through the years a tradition of holding down the cost of operation of the Mansion has been established through the custom of staffing the home with persons chosen from among volunteers from the state penitentiary at Parchman. The prisoners who are selected for this role at the Mansion are carefully monitored during their period of service. At the end of the Governor's term, they are frequently rewarded by being granted paroles or suspended sentences.

The absence of any other means of providing a staff for the Mansion makes the "trusty" system of house servants a necessity for any Governor and his family. It also offers a challenge for the Governor to see that the time of service in the Mansion is one of occupational therapy and job-training for the convicts, to fit them for a useful and productive role in the "free world" when they are released.

The thought of responsibilities like that for the convict-servants tempered some of my happy feelings of anticipation as my husband William prepared to assume his role as the 49th Governor of Mississippi on January 20, 1980.

Throughout his life, he has made the study of Mississippi and American history both his major hobby and recreation, as well as a continuing part of his preparation for the responsibilities of public life. Perhaps because he is a history student, his respect for tradition as a stabilizing and positive force in American life is all the greater.

To highlight that respect for tradition, William decided to have his inaugural at the historic Old Capitol. But as he and I moved into the Mansion, we did so with plans to establish a new tradition of utilizing hospitality at the Mansion as a force in leading Mississippi toward educational, economic and social progress.

To stress the new tradition, our first overnight guest at the Mansion was the celebrated Mississippi opera star, Miss Leontyne Price. After her first great success as an opera and concert star, Miss Price had returned to Mississippi for several concert performances, but she had never been accorded the recognition at an official function so well deserved by a concert artist of her commanding stature.

William asked me to call Miss Price personally with an invitation to sing the Star-Spangled Banner at the inauguration ceremony, and to be our official guest at the Mansion that night. As the newly inaugurated Governor commented in the preliminary to his inaugural address, after the thrilling experience of hearing Miss Price sing the National Anthem in the chamber where the Ordinance of Secession had been passed some 120 years before, "we (Mississippians) have honored ourselves through her rendition here today."

William Winter had no revolutionary program for Mississippi. Neither the temper of the time nor the financial resources of the state treasury offered the possibility of costly new programs. Fiscal conservatism had always been a hallmark of his governmental philosophy. He believed very firmly, however, that through effective leadership he could help bring economic and social progress to Mississippi through better education and the removal of the last vestiges of the long-time burden of racial discrimination and divisiveness.

I had been William's active partner in a lifetime of political campaigns, both winning and losing. I was to be his partner in this new leadership role for Mississippi, and my role as his hostess at the Mansion was to be a major part of that partnership. Our invitation to Leontyne Price was symbolic of the changes and of the active role of Mansion hospitality which we planned.

As our new residence, the Mansion was of course to be

the center for our family life, visits from family and long-time personal friends. It was also to be the site of almost daily working breakfasts, lunches and dinners for staff, legislators, and business and educational leaders involved in the Governor's efforts in these fields.

Beyond that, however, we planned a coordinated series of Mansion visits to help bring Mississippi to the attention of prominent and influential people the world over, and to help present a sampling of the views and ideas of national and world leaders to a cross-section of the people of Mississippi. In this overall effort our primary resource would be our greatest native asset—the qualities of individual Mississippians in and outside the state.

The plan was very simple. Prominent Americans, and sometimes citizens of other countries would be invited to the Mansion to be our overnight guests. In the evening they would be honored at an informal reception and dinner. After dinner the guest would talk informally on some topic related to his own experience and expertise, and then invite comments and questions from other guests at the dinner. To insure informality and a frank expression of opinion, all comments would be off the record, although very little in the way of "top secret" information was sought or expected.

To make the most of the opportunity offered by the presence of our guests, the dinners would be followed the next morning by a breakfast in the same pattern, but with a different set of guests. Where it appeared appropriate, and where the guest was willing, after the breakfast discussion, there would be a press conference at the Mansion for the guest.

As part of the overall Mansion guest program, the honoree would also be invited, if convenient to his or her plans, to visit other parts of the state in which he might be interested, or have some personal connection.

A major interest was featuring, as the honored guests,

native Mississippians—in most cases people who had made their mark outside the state but had retained strong ties at home and a continuing interest in the welfare of Mississippi. As the guest list shows, we did not discount people without Mississippi background or connection, but we felt that native Mississippians would be more effective messengers to Mississippi, and quite often more interesting to the cross-section of guests we would ask in for the dinners and breakfasts.

The overall program was a relatively simple one, but getting it into regular operation was by no means devoid of problems. Many of the guests were business and professional people for whom coming to Mississippi involved no financial problem but rather always a problem of scheduling. For others the scheduling had to be meshed with other travel, both to save time and limit costs, for there was—and is—no budget of state funds for the program.

The major cost of the visits is the food for the guests, who may number anywhere from fifty to eighty, depending on the time and circumstances of the visit. The food has to be squeezed out of the standard Mansion entertainment allowance. That procedure has proven to be a continuing problem, but in resolving it I have had the very effective help of two special members of the Mansion staff. Melba and Tommie Darras are two longtime friends and neighbors from Grenada who for many years operated a very successful restaurant there.

They had retired about a year and a half before we came to the Mansion. William and I proposed that they join us as housekeeper and chef at the Mansion, to direct their lifetime skills toward the overall goal of improving the quality of life in Mississippi, as they had for so many years improved the quality of the cuisine in Grenada. Melba and Tommie have been my partners in planning each of the dinners and breakfasts at the Mansion, both in regard to the quality of the food and the attractiveness of the setting, but also in the vitally important aspect of keeping down the cost. Without their marvelous help this effort would not have been possible.

In keeping with our long range goals for Mississippi, we have always had in mind a continuing effort to improve the image of Mississippi in the minds of the people who directly influence that image over the country. It has been our belief that the image in the national mind will most likely be an image of the Mississippians that national leaders come in contact with, both in and out of the state.

We believe that an exposure to a cross-section of Mississippians, as provided in our dinners at the Mansion, is good for the Mississippians so exposed, but most importantly it is good for the national leaders to meet and mix with prominent Mississippians on their own home ground. We believe that the mutual exposure has been beneficial for all concerned, but that it has been especially good for the image of our state.

This book is the result of many suggestions that I give a report about the experience of the dinners at the Mansion. I hope that the telling can help provide a clearer understanding of our effort to bring a better quality of life to Mississippians, and further contribute to our ever-present goal of creating a better understanding of Mississippi in the minds and hearts of people in every walk of life in our country.

Dean Rusk

I HAD never met Dean Rusk, but, from television appearances and news accounts, I had built an image of a reserved Southern gentleman of the old school, of a type I had come to respect as a girl growing up in north Mississippi. Mr. Rusk turned out to be one of those persons who lived up to a pre-conceived image.

He is gentle and easy to talk with, soft-spoken but articulate. His comfortable presence may help explain why he is one of the few men in American history who has served an entire eight years as Secretary of State, a job that seems to be more demanding with every passing year.

What I remember most about his visit is something he said only indirectly about foreign affairs. Somebody brought up the subject of the disruptive protests about the Vietnam War, and the sometimes obnoxious manners of the young people of the day.

"Be patient with the young people of this age," said Secretary Rusk, "and remember they have never known a glorious war."

I grew up exulting in the period of celebration of the glorious victories of World War II, and will always remember the marvelous sense of achievement that came with the end of the war. Now I also will remember Dean Rusk's words.

From his role as a student of Mississippi history, William likes to point out that Mississippians have always had an economic interest in American foreign policy throughout the history of the state. Too often, however, the immediate, day-to-day economic problems of earning a living have tended to preclude rational discussion of many foreign policy issues, and sometimes obscured the kind of analysis and decision which might have provided a clearer understanding of the relationship between Mississippi economic interests and American foreign policy.

Historically, the first rapid growth in Mississippi came with the expansion of cotton culture into the deep South from the southeastern Atlantic seaboard states. From its earliest days in America, cotton was heavily dependent upon an export market. Today cotton is no longer the king; but soybeans, the current major crop, are perhaps even more dependent upon foreign sales. Most of the major manufacturing industries which have come into Mississippi rely heavily upon imported raw materials or upon foreign sales of their finished products.

A major reason for Mississippians to be concerned about foreign policy is the fact that Mississippians have always been more than proportionately represented in both the officer corps and the enlisted personnel of the American armed forces. Mississippians are likely to continue to have a full share in American military involvement anywhere in the world.

Despite the compelling reasons to be interested in foreign policy, the overall issues have rarely been a major topic for public discussion in Mississippi. As Governor, William did not expect to try to focus on the topic, but he very strongly believes that there should be more interest and study in the field, at every level in the state.

Consequently, bringing to the Mansion people involved in American foreign policy decisions was a conscious effort toward focusing the attention of Mississippians on foreign policy issues. Two of our earliest overnight Mansion guests were the Ambassadors to the United States of Mexico and China. A number of study and trade missions from foreign countries have been invited for visits to William's office, and sometimes to lunch.

The concern about world affairs was the reason for asking Dean Rusk, who has had a lifetime of experience in foreign policy formulation and study, to be one of our first guests for dinner and discussion. Secretary Rusk came from the University of Georgia, where he is Professor of International Law.

Dean Rusk had been back in Georgia for ten years, but he was obviously still well versed on the current problems of American foreign policy, and well aware that there were still no easy answers for any of them. He expressed a polite disagreement with President Carter's then-recent characterization of the Soviet invasion of Afghanistan as the biggest threat to world peace since World War II.

"I wouldn't use that same rhetoric," Rusk said, and reminded us that the Cuban missile crisis while he was Secretary of State "was a pretty dangerous situation. . . . Each person lives through his own crisis," he said.

Many of the questions put to him were about the American hostages then being held in Iran, and his predictions proved to be remarkably accurate. He believed that they would be released, but that it might take still a long time more. For the time being, he said, the United States "pretty well will have to play for the breaks."

The former Secretary agreed with his fellow Georgian Jimmy Carter, about the boycott of the Olympic Games which had been put into effect.

"I find it very difficult to see our young people running, jumping and skipping with the Russians, under the Russian flag, while their people are shooting down Afghans not far away," he said, in the precise tones mellowed with a very recognizable Georgia accent.

Our guests for the Rusk dinner and breakfast were a

14

good mixture of business people, educators, religious leaders, state officials and housewives. As with any occasion, a few individuals seem to take the lead in asking questions and promoting the general discussion, but apparently their questions reflect those of the group who do not commit for most get an opportunity to say something if they have any desire to do so.

The procedure after our guests have retired from the dining rooms to the Rose Parlor is for William to introduce the guest, and to ask for a few words. Some talk for only five or six minutes before inviting questions, while others talk for as much as twenty minutes. William seems to enjoy the role of keeping the conversational interplay alive, although usually very little encouragement is needed. He asks questions himself from time to time, but generally his problem is to find a way to conveniently break up the discussion before it gets too late for some of the people to drive back home that night (or for the guest at the Mansion to have time enough to get some sleep before having a similar session at breakfast the next morning.)

Drawing up the guest list of Mississippi people for these affairs has never been easy, and will probably offer problems for the rest of our time at the Mansion. We have had the advantage of not having to follow rigid precedents, because there have been none, but this very lack of a defined protocol makes it inevitable that many people who—we know in retrospect—should have been invited get overlooked in the invitations.

We have tried to follow a procedure of including, through one event or another, state officials, including some in retirement, business and commercial leaders, religious leaders, educators, leading members of all the professions, longtime personal friends, and, of course, longtime political supporters. Those personal friends and political supporters are a pretty good cross-section of

Mississippi, and they always mean that the guests will be both interested and interesting.

Even within these broad limits, there are complications. An invitation to the Mansion is an important occasion for most Mississippians, but many of those we would like to have as guests live some distance from Jackson, and sometimes they cannot afford the time and monetary cost of a long drive and the accompanying hotel or motel expense. Consequently the guest list becomes sometimes unconsciously weighted with people from Jackson and the immediate vicinity.

When our guest of honor is a Mississippian, or with a special Mississippi background, we try to include family members and personal associates from back home. It makes the occasion a little more homelike and festive for all of us.

We have learned to check the mechanics of the invitation process, to make sure that there are no vacant spaces for occasions when we know that there are many more who would have liked to come. When our written formal invitations receive no reply, we follow up with a phone call—to make sure an invitation has not somewhere slipped through the postal cracks, to everyone's subsequent embarrassment.

Each invitation list is drawn up from the general lists mentioned above, with the help of one of my staff assistants, and with William's advice and specific suggestions. It is not unusual for him to issue a verbal invitation to someone he encounters along his daily appointment schedule, and he is usually very good about making sure that name gets immediately on the formal list, and that such invitations are not made after the formal invitations are out.

But, like many another wife, I am not immune from the unexpected dinner guest invited by the husband who forgets to notify the wife. I have found that a good staff, especially the chef and housekeeper, can make these occasions go almost unnoticed—even when they have to add a place at the table while the dinner is being served. It happens in the best of families, even at the Mansion.

Tea

TEA AT the Mansion can be very formal, served from an impressive silver service that once was part of the formal dinnerware of the Battleship Mississippi; or it can be very informal, handled by a combination of Mansion servants and volunteer friends who like to help us entertain in our historic structure.

Tea can also be an almost casual affair, more like punch and cookies than tea, but retaining the basic structure of being an instrument to show hospitality with both a limited time and a limited budget.

One of the first "mass" teas that we gave at the Mansion involved the top performers among the new generation of scholars in Mississippi, and there was a special reason for the occasion.

Recognition of Mississippians who have played a part in improving the quality of education in our state has been one of the major activities of the Governor's office and ceremonies and functions at the Mansion since William began his administration. His legislative program in all three years has featured efforts to improve both the administration and financing of education, but he has also felt a strong need to recognize those who are contributing to progress, and to praise them for the efforts which will benefit all the people of the state.

One April afternoon hundreds of high school valedictorians, most of them accompanied by one or both of their parents, and in some cases a teacher, came as especially invited guests for tea and cookies at the Mansion. Every valedictorian in the state had been asked to come for the visit, and receive a scholar's certificate from the Governor.

The line of young people seemed long to those of us dispensing handshakes and refreshments, but we were immediately pleased to see their obvious pleasure in being in the Mansion. It was only a small reward for a very productive use of their talents, but there seemed to be satisfaction in the realization that their efforts had been recognized by their Governor in asking them to the Mansion.

As a parent, however, I think I enjoyed most the sense of achievement and satisfaction of the parents who were on hand with their scholarly children. I managed to have a few words with many of them: "We are proud of your son (daughter)." The answer usually was, "We're proud, too."

Traditionally we are concerned with motivating children to take advantage of educational opportunity, but I do not believe that motivation will be fully in place until we have motivated parents to provide the moral support that will help the student stay in school and be a productive scholar as well. Our small contribution to honor their achievement, which we hope will become a regular custom, will also make a small contribution toward building parent motivation.

The reception for the valedictorians was the social highlight of an intensive two-day program which the Governor's office had arranged in cooperation with the Mississippi Academy of Sciences. On the night before there had been a dinner addressed by a Nobel Prize Winner, Dr. Arno Penzias, of the Bell Telephone laboratories. Dr. Penzias had been our overnight guest at the Mansion.

Before the valedictorians came to the Mansion they had attended a forum led by college student leaders who were reporting on their study of the needs for scientific and technological education in Mississippi, a subject highlighted by Dr. Penzias the night before.

Dr. Penzias, who is an orthodox Jew, came to us during

19

a time of strict dietary limits for persons of his faith, Passover. His meal at the banquet was brought to the hotel by some Jewish friends of ours who operate a delicatessen, but I had to provide the breakfast the next morning's Mansion breakfast, which we had expanded to include a number of local guests.

I talked to several Jewish friends about all of the details, and I think we met all the requirements. Dr. Penzias could not eat food from anything that had been used before, such as our regular china plates. We substituted paper and plastic, to meet that basic problem. Soft-boiled eggs had to be served in the shell, so I had to scout and borrow some egg cups when I discovered that they were not part of the dinnerware at the Mansion.

Everything went well, and Dr. Penzias was a delightful guest.

The Nobel laureate was not only very warm and personable, but he spoke in simple language with force and persuasion on the subject: "The Art of Asking Questions." I was very much interested in his discussion of the art of tying shoelaces, and took up the topic after we came back to the Mansion from the hotel where he had addressed the banquet.

Dr. Penzias reminded me that getting shoelaces tied properly had been a source of contention between parents and children for generations, usually because children could not readily learn the intricacies of a square knot or a granny knot. Somewhat facetiously I suggested that maybe we ought to make loafers without laces the standard wear for children.

"I really am serious about the problem," he replied. "It is so very important for a small child to have a good self-image and to feel that this is something that he can do well. There simply should not be this source of irritation between parents and children."

I have borrowed this simple theme from a Nobel Prize

physicist and used it several times in speaking to school and parent groups on my continuing theme of the importance of early childhood education.

This tea at the Mansion is the largest function related to education in the state, but the role of many of our overnight Mansion guests has been concerned with education. One of the early ones was Dr. David Mathews, who was Secretary of Health, Education and Welfare in the cabinet of President Gerald Ford. Dr. Mathews was first widely known as the very youthful but highly capable president of the University of Alabama, and he is now President of the Kettering Foundation. At the time he visited us he was President of the National Consortium for Public Policy Education, and acting as chairman of the Commission on the Future of the South, a project of the Southern Growth Policies Board, of which William would be chairman in 1982.

To have dinner and breakfast with Dr. Mathews, we invited a number of educators, but most of our guests were business and industrial leaders, and people in government. William knew that a discussion of the future of the South would feature economic topics, but that they would be related to education, and he wanted people other than educators to be involved in the discussion.

"The romanticism with Southerners is over," Dr. Mathews stated as he started the discussion. "There is a sense in the country that there is another new leadership in the South that is very different from the New South leadership. Our prosperity and our advances that were applauded just five years ago are looked on with a mixture of envy and maybe a sense of unjust entitlement . . . We look— by all of the indices that we use to categorize the country—pretty much like the country as a whole. In nearly every sector (of measurement) we are like the rest of the country."

Despite all of these evidences of "the Americanization of

21

Dixie" Dr. Mathews stressed that his report made it clear that "all was not sunny in the Sunny South." Two examples of peculiarly Southern problems were the lack of capital formation in the Southern economy, and the fact that there were far more Southern children living in homes at the poverty level than children in other sections of the country—30% of the nation's children live in the South, but 40% of America's poor children happen to be in the South.

I won't try to explain the discussion about capital formation, except to say that the gist of the agreed-upon solution was that we needed to find ways to retain in the South more of the wealth created in our farms and factories. Banking structures and tax laws may have to be changed so that all of this can be more easily accomplished. And, as with most major problems, there is no sure and certain way to achieve this capital formation.

The Commission on the Future of the South included a special task force on the Children of the South, with Mississippi represented by Mrs. Martha Stennis. The report was not completed at the time Dr. Mathews met with us, but he knew enough of its findings to make it clear that the South needed to be more concerned than ever about the future of its children, who were, after all, the future of the South.

"If you look at what's happening to children in the South now, the South of the 1980's looks more like the South of the 1930's than it does of the South we live in," Dr. Mathews said. He mentioned the 40% of the poor children, but added that "among the very poor children, those who are way down on the list, we have something of 75% of the children below the poverty level . . . Almost one million Southern children under five live in poor families."

He pointed out that there were counties in Mississippi and Alabama where the health statistics for children were worse than those for children in many other less developed countries. As he further described children's health conditions, ". . . in some Southern counties the most dangerous thing you can do is try to get born. But if you're lucky enough to make it, your chances of having some impairment are greater for the same reason that your chances of dying were greater."

Dr. Mathews listed a number of educational statistics which showed special problems as far as students in the South were concerned.

"The dropout rate in the South is higher than in the rest of the country," he pointed out, and "forty-two percent of the parents in the South have less than a high school education, as compared to thirty-four percent nationally," and he made it clear that he thought there was a correlation between the two facts.

Dr. Mathews' special interest in public policy education led to a very eloquent plea for a role for education in informing people about the issues relevant to public policy, especially in relation to issues critical to the South today.

"I want to argue that educational institutions in secondary education, the great colleges and universities with their continuing education divisions, the community junior colleges with their good link to the public, that they all take seriously the responsibility of educating adults for the quintessential responsibility of an adult in our society, which is not learning how to weave baskets or learning how to cook Chinese food, but how to execute the office of citizen."

After he was asked about the continuing education process for the general public, about how well the public could be informed about the issues of the day, Dr. Mathews said, "I'm worried about whether there are certain limitations in the media that are making it more difficult [to fully explain issues]. I think two of the greatest threats to an informed citizenry participating in the affairs of government are polling and the wired cities [for instance polling in connection with TV sets].

"The media, by its very nature, has limited space. Have you ever tried to explain federal policy on recombinant DNA or the intricacies of the welfare system in 45 seconds? . . . One of the most interesting things that could happen in education would be a combination between education and radio and TV and the newspaper folks about how the public comes to understand."

I think that the message that came to me from the David Mathews' visit was the complete relationship between education and economic progress in the South. Health and our general cultural pattern are just one step away from being as closely related.

It's almost part of a general educational effort. The young valedictorians in their bright spring dresses and neatly pressed summer suits had come to Jackson as part of that education process that a Governor can help lead. These young leaders will be a little bit further along than their parents, and it will gradually show up in accelerated growth in the quality of life in our state.

The whole effort is well worth spilled punch, styrofoam cups instead of crystal cups, cookie crumbs and an occasional crushing handshake. It is the process which we have to make work.

Volunteers and Visitors

AS THIS account has probably made clear, the Mississippi Governor's Mansion is in part a private residence, an official state public building, and a state museum. Through long custom, staffing the Mansion has been done through the cooperation of state agencies like the Highway Patrol; through volunteer assistance, through the services of inmates assigned from the state penitentiary at Parchman; and by the Governor himself.

The mission, as I see it, of the Mansion as a public building could not be met without the generous volunteer help of a group of Jackson ladies who serve as docents. The dictionary defines docents as persons who conduct groups through museums or art galleries. The Mansion is neither a museum, nor an art gallery, the ladies who serve as Mansion guides are fully entitled to that special title of docent. On regular visiting days, and on a number of special occasions, they shepherd visitors through the Mansion to reach a total of more than 25,000 each year.

Without the help of the docents, all volunteers, it would be impossible to handle so many people with a minimum of disruption and damage and wear to the Mansion furnishings. The work of the docents is coordinated by the curator of the Mansion, assigned by the State Department of Archives and History in the light of its responsibility for an historic state building.

The normal work of the Mansion is carried on while the tours are conducted. Impromptu tours guided by one of the regular Mansion staff come up frequently, sometimes several times a day. These often result when delegations have come to see the Governor at his Mansion office, and they have the time to take a tour either before or after their meeting with the Governor.

The regular public tours are conducted Tuesday through Friday morning, 9:30 to 11:30, all through the year. The volunteer ladies have all qualified as docents by participating in a course of instruction arranged by the Department of Archives and History—about the plans and furnishings of the Mansion, about the actual history of the house and some of the people who have lived here. Fact has been separated from fiction in the descriptions the guides give the visitors, and in their responses to questions. Of course, no one is ever able to anticipate all the questions, but the docents handle them all with great aplomb.

Thanks to the large number of volunteers, most of the docents have to be on duty no more than one morning a month. Docents also are on hand for the use of the Mansion by various statewide organizations, who can arrange to use the Mansion for teas and receptions on two afternoons each week.

As a girl at Senatobia, I grew up in my grandmother's home with fireplaces in every room, and mantels from which to hang Christmas stockings.

When our children were small, we lived in a house that did not have mantels or fireplaces of any sort, and there consequently seemed to be something missing at Christmas. I would take the children to the Old Capitol, which always has a large Christmas tree in the rotunda, with the bannisters of the surrounding spiral staircase covered with greenery.

These Christmas visits always brought a feeling of the security and comfort of an old-fashioned Christmas. I determined to carry the idea further at the Mansion.

Our first Christmas at the Mansion was the occasion for some lovely decorations arranged by all of us, staff and volunteers. For the Rose Parlor downstairs there was a traditional formal tree decorated with gold bows and nosegays of dried flowers, with lace and baby's breath and tiny white lights. Upstairs in the central hallway, we had a chidren's tree—decorated with cookies made in our kitchen by Melba Darras—gingerbread men and gingerbread animals. At the base were some old-fashioned children's toys, including a number which had belonged to my children. I even added the old stuffed teddy bear, one arm and all, which had belonged to me as a child and was later used by my children.

We put on the tree, but never lighted, the small white candles which were used on Christmas trees a long time ago. Larger candles, in safer settings, were scattered throughout the house, blended with pine cones and poinsettias.

Both to fit the occasion and to make the Mansion more accessible to office workers in downtown Jackson, I came up with the idea of candlelight tours in the twilight and early darkness from 5 p.m. to 7 p.m. These tours were arranged for four afternoons in the two weeks before Christmas.

Schools and colleges in the area were pleased to have their choirs sing Christmas carols from the front porch, or from bleachers set up near the outdoor tree. At one end of the parlor were refreshments for each visitor—wassail and ginger cookies—something very simple, but adding a festive note. Between four and five thousand people came for the first candlelight tours, and the crowds have grown each year.

Functions such as these, which have become annual events, have been well received by many friends that we know, and strangers who have become friends that we met when they visited on one of these tours. Mississippians love the old house, and regard it as part of their state and part of their heritage. They tell us that they want the Governor to live in a house that they can be proud of, and one that they can show visitors with pride as a Mississippi instition.

Keeping it pretty and clean and still functioning is more than a dawn-to-dusk job, of course. One night, when a TV crew was filming some scenes involving "Miss USA" and a Mansion tour, I was downstairs with themuntil two in the morning.

Sometimes I laughingly say that I should have taken a degree in hotel management rather than history. But history comes in handy in a historic home.

In arranging for our overnight Mansion guests, I think we use a little bit of both backgrounds. These overnight guests always spend the night in the historic areas. We place flowers in their rooms, even if it is no more than a single rosebud, or a blooming African violet. We always have fruit in the rooms occupied by guests, and a small silver dish of candy.

There is a guest book to be signed, to record the guest's signature and where each person stayed. The guests can also satisfy their own curiosity as to who had been there before them.

One of the housemen has a special duty to get upstairs and turn down the beds while the guests are at dinner, to provide a little more at-home feeling. In the morning, at the time requested, a coffee tray and a newspaper are brought up to the overnight visitor.

We have place cards for all but our smallest dinners, and our curator, Kitty Czarnieci, writes the names beautifully in calligraphy. We have no major protocol problems in the sittings, either above or below the salt. But the person who knows the most about the guests—whether they have been previously acquainted or share special interests—is the man who already knows virtually all the guests in advance: William Winter.

28

So, if you take a last minute peek before the guests enter, you are likely to find the Governor of Mississippi setting up the place cards in the Mansion dining room.

Leontyne Price

IN APRIL of 1981, William Carey College in Hattiesburg demonstrated the remarkable resourcefulness of that institution when it arranged a 75th Anniversary Convocation to award honorary degrees to three outstanding Mississippi women.

William Carey was for many years a women's college at Hattiesburg supported by the Baptist Church, little known outside of south Mississippi, but responsible for the quality education of several generations of fine young Mississippi women. In recent years it has met the severe challenge faced by private institutions of higher learning with an aggressive adaptation to the changing conditions of the times. Men are now admitted as students, and local branches of the school have extended its enrollment.

On the 75th Anniversary it was fitting that William Carey honor Miss Lucile Parker, the art teacher who had inspired several generations of students to fully appreciate the world of art, from masterworks to modern, and also to explore the development of their own artistic talents.

The broad scope and potential of William Carey was demonstrated, however, when the convocation also awarded honorary degrees to Mississippi's two greatest living artists, novelist Eudora Welty and soprano Leontyne Price. Miss Welty and Miss Price not only happen to be Mississippi's most outstanding artists without regard to sex, but they also happen to be accepted as foremost in their field among all women in the country. In securing the joint acceptance of the honorary degree by these two great women artists, William Carey gained for itself an academic event sought but never achieved by other institutions, including many of the Ivy League schools of the East.

Leontyne Price's return to Mississippi offered an opportunity for her to accept a standing invitation to be our guest of honor at a Mansion dinner. We turned the dinner into an affair honoring all three of the ladies to be recognized at William Carey, and we used it as an event to celebrate Mississippi's achievement in the arts, and the potential for further achievement.

William and I not only wanted to join William Carey College in honoring these three great ladies, but we also wanted to honor the state of arts in Mississippi and among Mississippians. To help carry this idea forward, we included in our guest list William Ferris, Director of the Center for the Study of Southern Culture at Ole Miss, and Willie Morris, the Yazoo City native who is now writer-in-residence at the Journalism Department at Ole Miss.

Describing the occasion is still a difficult task, for all of us were affected by the transcendent occasion which it became. We asked about 60 people to be our guests, and would have asked more if space had permitted. For large dinners such as this, we begin with the table for 16 in the formal dining room. Four tables for eight are arranged in the adjacent Gold parlor (with the folding doors open). In addition, we placed two more tables for eight in the rear of the broad center hallway, adjacent to the open door of the dining room.

The gardens at the Mansion have very lovely flowers, but to make sure that the main table was at its best I added several varieties of spring flowers from the yard of our home on Crane Boulevard, supplemented by dogwood blossoms, then at the height of their beauty. The guests assembled in the Rose Room on the west side of the Mansion, where wine, tomato juice and hors d'oeuvres were served.

Leontyne Price is a stately, regal beauty, with a presence that fully complements her glorious voice. She was the center of attention from the moment when she first came downstairs to join us, but William made the after-dinner talk and discussion something for her to hear rather than to remain, so to speak, on center-stage. The topic of the evening was Southern culture, and Mississippi culture in particular.

Bill Ferris, who taught at Jackson State and Yale before he came back to Mississippi to organize the Center for Southern Culture at Ole Miss, was asked to talk about the culture of the South, its history, and how we could relate it to the future progress that we all seek.

"We've begun in the spirit of what Eudora Welty has called a sense of place, in trying to understand what really shapes us so deeply," Bill said. "Not only in fiction, but I think in all of our lives, we've talked about the places we've come from. Somehow being from Mississippi, being from Laurel, being from Vicksburg makes a very distinctive and special part of who we are.

"So places are important, and it is also what we do with places that is important. I think perhaps the perspective of the year 2000, when we look back on this century, the one place that has inspired and created art and celebrated place and loved it most deeply has been the South. Within the South certainly no state has produced more of which we can be proud than Mississippi. As a folklorist, I think one of those traditions coming out of our state that has been most exciting to me has been music."

Then Bill, unabashed in the presence of one of the world's greatest singing voices, took up his guitar and illustrated his points with both songs and snatches of songs. They are the kind known as American over the world, but actually all with a direct tie to Mississippi, ranging from B.B. King and Jimmie Rodgers to Muddy Waters and Elvis Presley. Leontyne and Eudora seemed to enjoy it as much as all the rest of us.

William introduced Leontyne by saying that one of the highest honors he had ever received was having her sing "The Star-Spangled Banner" at his inauguration, which we both will remember as long as we live.

Leontyne responded by saying, "There has never been a more important reason for my coming home to sing than it was for your inauguration, which I think is wonderfully and scintillatingly obvious to all of us, not just in the state but in the general heartbeat of progress in our country."

She added that coming home was always an expression of a continuation of her "Mama and Daddy." (In keeping with that spirit, we also had as our guest in the Mansion George Price, her brother, who is a retired General of the United States Army.) She also spoke of the friendship of her family with that of the Alexander Chisholms of Laurel. (Mrs. Jean Chisholm Lindsey was also one of our guests.)

"Our roots are based on all things that are fundamentally strong and positive, particularly if you're a Mississippian, and this has to do with a certain palpitation, a certain quality, a certain way of doing things with a pace that makes progress with us a standing thing. There's nothing instant about it, but it's the hard work that's put into it that makes it go and stand and will be very difficult to wipe away."

Most of us had seen the national television report of a few days before, where Leontyne had slightly altered the words of "God Bless America" to sing a plea before a U.S. Senate Committee to support funds for the arts and humanities. She reminded us of that, and said that now "I would like to sing it in its original form, being very obvious to fall back on what I always hope will solve all of our problems and hopefully many others." She then sang, from a corner of the Rose Parlor of the Governor's Mansion, "God Bless America."

Hearing it in this special setting was an overwhelming experience, still impossible for me to adequately describe.

After the first burst of applause, there was an appreciative, respectful silence.

William said that he could not attempt to say anything after the stirring experience of the rendition, and after a moment he called on Eudora Welty for a word.

Eudora was also deeply moved by the emotional nature of the event: "What can I say, except that with the greatness and beauty and feeling and strength of her voice she encompasses what any artist feels inside and perhaps can never express, but which *she* does."

Eudora and Leontyne had met for the first time because they both had roles in the Winter inauguration. Eudora was the most prominent of a number of outstanding Mississippi natives, most of whom now live outside the state, who had appeared in a symposium "Mississippi in the 1980's" the afternoon before the inauguration. Inauguration morning, Leontyne had expressed a desire to meet Eudora, and their meeting and greeting was a special highlight of the whole day for those who happened to be near them when they were brought together at the Inaugural brunch.

On the day following the Mansion dinner, we had arranged a luncheon for Leontyne which we hoped would have a direct impact on support for music in the Jackson area—friends and benefactors of the Jackson Symphony Orchestra and Opera South, for instance. About 50 people were present for this luncheon, which followed the pattern of the evening before.

After Leontyne had spoken to the group following the luncheon, I took the liberty of asking her to sing "God Bless America" again, and she did, with the same deep and thrilling tone. The audience response was like the night before. As one of my friends among the guests wrote in a bread and butter letter later that day:

. . . thank you from the bottom of
every chamber of my heart for letting

34

me share in the transcendent occasion
which was today . . . Her voice is so
marvelous—if the Ku Klux Klan could
really hear her, they would disband immediately . . .

Leontyne made herself available for a brief news conference, and then she hurried away to Hattiesburg and
William Carey, accompanied by her brother, and her
manager, a personable gentleman named Hubert
Dilworth.

William and I were planning to join them at dinner and
the convocation at William Carey later that evening, but a
last minute complication arose. Fairly late in the afternoon, I was dressed for our flight to Hattiesburg when
William called to say that the Legislature was still in session, and that he could not possibly leave. I told him that I
would go in time for the dinner, and he planned to come
down two hours later for the convocation.

Flying down, I had a few moments to rest from what
had been a thoroughly enjoyable, but hectic twenty-four
hours. I thought that it wasn't absolutely necessary for
William to make a special trip down just for the convocation. He was tired, he also had to work on a special address to the Legislature for the following Friday morning,
and he might be neglecting some legislative responsibility
by leaving. As far as he knew, he had no essential part on
the program. When the plane landed I called back to
Jackson from the airport and asked him, "Why don't you
just stay in Jackson?" I think it was with obvious relief that
he took my advice.

Almost immediately I discovered that I had to take on a
special job in the absence of my husband.

When I reached William Carey College, Dr. J. Ralph
Noonkester, President, very kindly understood William's
problem, but he explained that William had been assigned
a part on the program for the dinner as well as the con-

vocation. So at the dinner I wound up giving an official "welcome-to-Mississippi" to all the out-of-staters present.

I had innocently expected to be a part of the audience at the convocation, enjoying the proceedings with no concerns, similar to that of the hostess for the night before. Dr. Noonkester told me that William was expected to give the invocation to open the program.

Fortunately, as a graduate of the University of Mississippi, like my husband, I could appropriately wear the academic cap and gown that had been reserved for him. The program seemed to go well enough, even with the addition of my unrehearsed part, though I was amazed at the strange turn of events.

Miss Price was chosen to make the address in response to the award of the degrees, by designation of the other two honorees. She spoke beautifully, and her words in praise of the example and heritage of her mother were simple truths that reached everybody. Once again her remarks built up to an even greater climax. In the quiet auditorium, she sang, *a capella*, "This Little Light of Mine." No operatic air she had ever sung in any opera house in the world reached a more ecstatic or appreciative audience.

I returned late that Thursday night to the Mansion, tired but still thrilled at the experience of the two nights and the day between. It would have been nice to have a rest, but we had new guests at the Mansion for that Friday night — Senator and Mrs. John Glenn. It was far better to be at home in the morning to see that arrangements for the Glenns were complete, and to join the Governor in going to the airport to greet the famous astronaut, now respected statesman.

Welty-Alexander

EUDORA WELTY has earned a place as one of the great American writers of this century. She has been awarded the Pulitzer Prize for literature, the National Book Award, and dozens of other high honors for novels and short stories, and she has remained through the years simply a marvelous person and good citizen of Jackson.

We are proud of her as a Mississippian, and also as a personal friend. She honored William by presenting a paper at his inaugural symposium, and she has been a guest at several or so of our Mansion functions honoring other persons. We have had the good fortune to be able to honor her as hosts for two dinners and a luncheon to celebrate some of her recent achievements.

The first of these occasions was to honor the judges for the Eudora Welty Americana Award, an important project on public television. One of the judges was our own Margaret Walker Alexander, another was Chloe Aaron, an official of the Public Broadcasting Service, and the third was Dr. Edward Stasheff, Professor Emeritus at the University of Michigan, and the former producer of the Ed Sullivan show who set up the educational television system in Israel. When we learned that the judges would meet in Jackson with Miss Welty, we asked them to be our guests with her at a Mansion dinner.

William was out of the state at the time, but the evening went very well. Dr. Stasheff seemed to be much impressed by it all, and he was nice enough to send a thank-you note in the form of a little verse:

ODE (OWED?) TO 'THE GOVERNOR'S LADY'
To a stranger, visiting from the North
Life in Mississippi seems like a dream.
Hosts and hostesses graciously come forth
To prove that old traditions *are* what they seem.
The centuries of Southern Hospitality
(Old legends acclaimed in song and story)
From Myth and legend are turned to Reality—
Another source of Mississippi's glory.
Where else could this visitor, passing through,
Find that here wildest dreams come true:
Have drinks with a Medal of Merit winner
And take the Governor's Lady in to dinner!

Our special dinner for Miss Welty came a few weeks later in recognition of the award to her of the Presidential Medal of Freedom, an award which honored her greatness as a writer as well as her qualities as a person.

We were able to have several members of her family as guests, as well as some of our mutual friends in Jackson, such as Charlotte Capers and Mr. and Mrs. Reynolds Cheney.

The conversation and the company, as well as the food, were very pleasant, but the highlight of the evening came after dinner when we went across the hall to the Rose Parlor, and Eudora read a passage from her book, *The Optimist's Daughter.* It was about the heroine Laurel, and her dream that she was with Phil again.

People who have not heard Eudora Welty read have missed one of the great experiences of their lives, for Eudora is a marvelous perfectionist in the now almost forgotten art of Reading. Many years ago it was taught in school as "Expression."

Eudora Welty's characters best come alive in their reading by Eudora Welty. When she finds the right audience, she loves to read—sometimes her short stories and sometimes passages from the novels.

After the reading that night I realized what we had lost by not having a tape recorder to make a permanent record of the event—something we have managed to do for almost all our later dinners.

Another great woman writer also lives in Jackson, and we have been proud to honor her as one of the most illustrious persons of our state. "Margaret Walker Alexander Day" was held when she retired from her active role at Jackson State University. The Jackson Urban League Guild organized the tribute, and our part was to give a luncheon at the Mansion.

Margaret Walker Alexander's *Jubilee* has been called the black *Gone With the Wind*, but it is really much more than that—a powerful story that delineates the part of black people from the period of slavery into the first freedom. I believe, along with many others, that it has become an important part of American literary history.

Mrs. Alexander is also a poet of great ability. Perhaps her best known poem is "For My People." Her family has been involved in black education in Mississippi for more than a century, and her long tenure at Jackson State and her active role in civic and cultural affairs has made her a major influence in our state.

She did not present a formal paper or speech at our luncheon, but her remarks during the affair and afterwards mirrored many of the points she had made at the Inaugural Symposium on January 21, the day before William was inaugurated:

"We need to stretch our minds and stretch our faith in order to accommodate our thinking to the problems of our systemic crises so that we can meet the challenges of the 1980's," she said. "We need to understand the Einsteinian principles of unity in diversity—a racial and cultural diversity as well as an illimitable universe. . .

"Then we can better understand our pluralistic universe," she continued. "We need to develop international understanding and peace on the basis of such unity in cultural and racial diversity. We need to develop religious tolerance so that we can respect all religious faiths, and know that God is truly the Father/Mother of all mankind, and that every man is our brother, every woman is our sister, and every child has the light of God and all human personality is holy and divine."

Mrs. Alexander is forthright and outspoken, and certainly never at a loss for words. She speaks with such conviction, and with such a record of scholarship and achievement in her background, that anything she says commands respect.

The Margaret Walker Alexander Day luncheon included a number of dignitaries, some of whom were in town for a dinner at Jackson State that night, but I was especially pleased that we could include most of her children and grandchildren, as well as her husband Firnist. Also among the guests was the well known writer, Lerone Bennett, Jr., who is senior editor of **Ebony** magazine, but best known that day as a native of Clarksdale.

William and I believe very firmly that helping to show our pride in our cultural leaders and our cultural assets is good for all of us as Mississippians, and also good for our efforts to improve the national image of Mississippi.

Flowers

WILLIAM NEVER promised me a rose garden, but one of the very attractive "perks" of life in the Governor's Mansion is a lovely little rose garden in the backyard of the grounds.

There are about fifty rose bushes in beds edged in brick, connected by a pathway made of clam shells. The roses begin to bloom in early April, and sometimes continue into December, with the loveliest blossoms coming in both the spring and the fall. They provide one of the greatest pleasures that I have known in many years of politics.

The roses are Tiffany, Tropicana, Ivory Fashion, Color Magic, Double Delight, Mr. Lincoln, and Mississippi. With such a wide variety of color, it gives us a chance to place them in different rooms of the Mansion with colors that match or complement the room.

Thanks to care in the past, and wonderful help from volunteers from the Central Rose Society, the rose garden was well-established when I arrived. We have had to replace a few of the bushes, but they are always lovely, and we have enjoyed and loved every blossom.

In fact, we have even saved the blooms that are spent, and used the petals for our very own potpourri. For Christmas, 1981, we had a luncheon in honor of the docents who are such indispensable help in showing the Mansion, and by each place card there were sachets filled with Mansion potpourri. The potpourri has become a tradition now, and we keep it in various places all around the house. We have made politics and roses go together rather well, I think.

This lovely old house deserves flowers every day. To supplement our roses, Melba Darras and I go out along the roadside from time to time to bring in wild flowers that are in season. We especially like the black-eyed susans, and sometimes mix them with a little goldenrod. We limit the sprigs of goldenrod in respect to the guests who may have allergies, but so far we have noticed no adverse reactions.

Perhaps this is because all the rooms in the Mansion are so large and airy to begin with. All flower arrangements almost of necessity have to be large. The dining room table is kept at its maximum length of fourteen feet, in order to seat sixteen, and consequently the type of arrangement that a person would use in the average home would look lost in this room. We have to think big in terms of arrangements, and big bowls filled with roses and Queen Anne's lace have become my favorites.

Our source of Queen Anne's lace is still the patches of road-side growth to be found in abundance in the Jackson area. Melba and I make these trips for flowers sometimes by ourselves, but at times I go with a member of the security detail as driver. Shepherding a female flower gatherer is not exactly the role model which our patrolmen-on-special-assignment seek to establish, so flower-gathering is probably not a preferred task.

One day I was cutting Queen Anne's lace alongside a road when I noticed that my driver, George Henderson, was standing by the car, but that his head was tucked down as though he was trying to be somewhere else. I later learned that he was afraid one of his colleagues from the Highway Patrol Academy would drive by and see him standing there watching me cut flowers. He is a tall, (distinguished looking) black man who stands out either in a crowd or alone, so there was not much chance of his being overlooked as he patiently waited for the wildflowers to be gathered.

In addition to Queen Anne's lace and Goldenrod, we

sometimes find more exotic items like wild Verbena and Indian Paintbrush, and some other flowers which we can't positively identify. I like to use flowers such as these, which I know are native to the state, and also because the flower-gathering expeditions are lighter on the budget than ordering from a florist.

Melba has been a great help with the floral duties, not only because of her endless energy, but because she has a natural flare for arranging flowers, and revitalizing sprays and arrangements. She has quite often taken an arrangement from the dining room table, put it in the refrigerator, freshened it with a few new flowers that are available from the yard or gardens or brought in by friends—most often hydrangeas, forsythia or jonquils—and come up with an entirely new arrangement that impresses everyone.

Our volunteer flower help includes two professionals, Pat Cothren and Cleta Ellington, who take on a major role when there is a large banquet or dinner that requires flower arrangements at a dozen other spots besides the big dining table. They have established a workshop in the basement, to which they sometimes have to bring their children who play or eat cookies while their mothers are busy working. The Mansion pays the retail prices for flowers and supplies, but Pat and Cleta donate their services.

I have noticed that the tourists who come in during the public visiting hours at the Mansion almost always comment on the flowers, just as do dinner and luncheon guests. We like to have pretty green leaves in the fireplaces and on the foyer table— quite often an arrangement of magnolia leaves, which are available the year round from trees on the grounds of state buildings.

In the fall and winter we usually have some dried flowers for the bedrooms upstairs, but even then we try to include potted plants like the African violets that I can grow in our personal quarters, where the curtains and

43

draperies are not so heavy, and more sunlight can be allowed into the room. We always try to have something green and growing in the Mansion so that it will be more homelike.

Orange and yellow nasturtiums are a very good contrast, however, and each spring I have planted some in a little space near the rose garden. I plant the seeds myself—something I learned from my grandmother. I have always loved these little herbal flowers, perhaps because they remind me of my girlhood home.

Perhaps the highlight of our use of the garden and flowers in connection with Mansion entertainment came in June, 1981, with a legislative garden party. It was necessary for the Governor to call the members of both the House and Senate back to Jackson for a briefing on what had become something of a financial crisis in state affairs. Because it was a one day trip, it seemed a convenient time for the wives of most of the members to come to Jackson with their husbands, so I planned an entertainment for them that would be interesting and relaxing, but inexpensive, and a dinner in the evening for the entire group.

While the members were being briefed at the temporary Capitol at Central High School, I took their wives to Highland Village, a Jackson shopping center to which we had been invited for a wine and cheese party and fashion show, thanks to the Sundowner Restaurant and Maison Weiss. Highland Village furnished us with a red London double-decker bus, which is one of their local trademarks. It turned out to be an unusually hot day for June, and English buses have no air conditioning, but quick trips kept that from being a major problem.

When our legislator-guests and their wives began to arrive about six p.m. at the Mansion, we had tables and chairs set up for almost three hundred people in the garden. The weather forecast was for rain, and we heard of showers in several other parts of the city. Fortunately the rain held off and we did not have to bring our guests indoors. The moon and stars were out by the time the party was over.

We served buffet style from a table under the portico which we use as a family entrance at the rear of the Mansion. There was a separate table from which Tommie Darras carved beef. From the buffet we had marinated vegetables, a squash casserole, shrimp and rice, chicken breasts, and homemade rolls. There was a dessert table farther out in the yard among the dining tables, from which the guests could choose baklava, pies and cakes, as well as demi-tasse.

Jack Jones' group with straw hats and striped coats played New Orleans' style jazz from the gazebo, and a combination of candles and hurricane lighting made a colorful setting.

In my view, however, the highlight was a centerpiece on each of the several dozen tables made up largely of wildflowers that Melba and I had cut from the edge of various highways. Along with roses, daisies and hydrangea from the garden itself, there were Queen Anne's lace, wild verbena, black-eyed susans and three or four other attractive plants that technically might have been called weeds, but which we thought were very pretty.

I wanted William to be aware, and I hope he made it clear to members of the Legislature, that we had not spent any money on flowers. We also made our own containers—baskets made of twigs and moss. After most of the guests had left, we joined in with the staff and a few special friends who had stayed, in folding up the chairs and tables and getting everything inside, from the biggest evening entertainment (in numbers of people) that we had held at the Mansion garden.

Southern Living

WHEN WILLIAM was growing up, he remembers that just about every farm family in Mississippi took *The Progressive Farmer,* Mississippi-Alabama edition. It had a lot of good farm information, it was cheap, and it was interesting to read. Besides that, it had been founded by a professor at Mississippi A&M, Dr. Tait Butler, even though its success had come after he left Mississippi.

For the past fifteen years, I have been reading *Southern Living,* a publication of the Progressive Farmer Company that has become identified with the growing quality of life all over the South. Some may say that *Southern Living* is too bland, but I think it is just the right blend of the flavor of the most enjoyable aspects of the Southern lifestyle. It is no accident that such a quality publication has become the most popular magazine in our region.

As one who is also interested in the economic progress that makes possible some of the life styles depicted in *Southern Living,* I am extremely proud of the fact that this Southern publication has been described as the most successful magazine venture of the past twenty-five years. My only regret is that it blossomed in Alabama instead of Mississippi.

Southern Living is perhaps the most exceptional financial success story in all the recent history of the South. In less than fifteen years, the company has grown from a ten million to a one million dollar business. At a time when many national magazines are ceasing publication, *Southern Living* has reached the largest circulation of regional

46

magazines in the world. It has twice the circulation of *Sunset*, its counterpart on the Pacific Coast.

An interesting aspect of the growth is that today the fastest circulation gains are in urban areas of northern states, even though, in the interest of concentration for advertisers, no special campaign has been made for outside-the-South circulation.

Until he came to the Mansion for a visit, I didn't know that Emory Cunningham, the President of the Progressive Farmer Company, and the man generally credited with the making *Southern Living* such a great success, had a Mississippi background. He grew up in Kansas, Alabama, just across the Mississippi line from Itawamba county. He first went to college at Perkinston Junior College, and he has a lot of Mississippi friends from that time before World War II. Mr. Cunningham turned out to be a good Southern neighbor, with many ideas similar to ours about improving the quality of life in the South.

I have to confess, however, that both Melba Darras and I were a little concerned about the reaction to our menu and service from the man who presides over the *Southern Living* kitchens and personally checks so many of furnishings and home displays that are featured each month in the magazine. He and his wife Jean seemed pleased with it all, however, and I trust they found that the Mansion and its hospitality lived up to the standards of *Southern Living*.

Emory Cunningham is proud of the success of both *Progressive Farmer* and *Southern Living*, but he is even prouder of the ways in which the South is changing and growing. He quoted from a book by Willie Morris which his company had published: "I am a Southerner. I like the feel of those words. I could no more be otherwise than I could change my outer skin or change the color of my eyes."

Then the publisher added his own words:

"Well, Willie Morris is not alone. There are an awful lot of people and I think most of us in this room, who share

47

those sentiments. I believe there is a growing number of people that feel that way, both native born and adopted Southerners. Both black and white are feeling that way more and more. I'm proud of it and I think it's an extremely important thing for us to nurture and enhance and develop the best of the qualities of Southern living."

Mr. Cunningham's optimism about the South, and the great record that *Southern Living* has gained in becoming the favorite publication of the Southern middle class, has not blinded him to the continuing problems of our region:

"For a long time we carried the burden of race. I think we've laid that burden down. I don't by any means mean to say everything is perfect. But I think we've broken the barrier and there's no longer the burden on us, on our backs as it was at one time.

"We still don't understand in the South how expensive ignorance is. We keep talking about education being expensive. I think if we think education costs too much, just try ignorance and find out about cost.

"In the South we have a lot of contradiction, but one of the great paradoxes and one of the things that makes us distinctive is our interest in land, our love of the land. But by the way we treat it, you might think that we hated it.

"If you drive some of the highways and just see some of the developments, you're going to say the people here don't love the land, they don't even respect it."

Mr. Cunningham cited the beauty of highways in North Carolina as an example of relatively simple steps that could accomplish a great deal.

"You may do what you want to do, back of the strips along the highway, but when you drive along the highway in North Carolina, the adjacent woods and all aren't bothered."

William expressed his appreciation for the role of *Southern Living* in helping to create an informed public opinion.

"We've tried," Mr. Cunningham responded. "If you read *Southern Living* you know that we never editorialize. We don't preach on these subjects. We don't offer opinions about them at all. What we try to do is to find examples of enlightened development where people have done a good job of developing land or designing a building. We try to portray that in a way that will serve as an example to other Southern people.

"We don't preach about saving the rivers, but we try to present the rivers in a way . . . that will encourage people to use them. . . . If the rivers and lakes and seacoast are saved, they'll be saved by people who use them and care.

"We believe that if you can get a man and a woman or a child and his parents started with a vegetable garden they've gotten something to communicate about. Growing that garden might help to hold that family together better than something we could write about of a counseling nature. The same applies to homes and design and cooking."

Mr. Cunningham complained, with a smile, that few people realized how difficult it was to combine good writing with good home economics. (He pointed out that his company probably employed more home economists than any other private employer in the country.)

"You don't know what sort of trouble you can get in if you publish a recipe and it turns out that you said half a tablespoon of salt when you meant half a teaspoon.

"Your instructions have got to be clear and concise, so that you don't get a telephone call from a lady who says, 'I've got out all of this stuff, I've bought all of this, and it's spread out all over the kitchen. I don't know what to do next'."

Mr. Cunningham revealed that they do not develop recipes within the company kitchens. Every one used comes originally from a reader, but all of them are tested at least one time before they are published.

He is very fervent in his belief that a continuing improvement in the quality of Southern living will be self-productive of an even higher quality.

"Good schools and good government and open spaces and a respect for the land, the water and the environment that we've been talking about . . . will bring in the kind of industry that brings human resources as well as capital, and upgrades the place that it moves into."

Advertising the resource won't be necessary, he said: "In our mobile society there's going to be such a lot of people that know about our (higher quality). They're going to come rushing here."

The psychic reward of building a better quality of life was something that he continually stressed. "Paying your civic dues, contributing to the country and building it along with profitability, is . . . part of the free enterprise system. . . . We really do need to get a different viewpoint than we've had in the past on that whole subject."

Emory Cunningham told us how people in Birmingham had said they couldn't afford to clean up the air, but now they realized they could not afford not to. I think the message of *Southern Living* and its success is that the South cannot afford *not* to consciously work for a higher quality of Southern life, and that all of us have a responsibility in that work.

The Arts At the Mansion

AS IT may be obvious to anyone reading this book, artists of all descriptions have formed the largest number of the people we have entertained at the Mansion—both performing artists and those who write, draw or paint.

Great singers like Leontyne Price are entitled to the biggest billing, perhaps, but we have not ignored salutes to some of the great folk artists of our time who make Mississippi their home, or are Mississippi natives.

Jerry Clower, the Amite County native who now makes his home in Yazoo City, is a story teller in the great line of American performing artists who have moved from Chautauqua tents to television. We had a reception and a dinner to honor him, and I suspect the laughter could be heard up and down Capitol Street!

Muddy Waters is an even more legendary figure of American folk music. He was born in Rolling Fork, but grew up in the north end of the Delta on the Stovall Plantation. Muddy Waters came back home to appear at the Delta Blues Festival in Greenville in 1981, but he also came to Jackson for a reception in the Governor's Mansion, and for a chance to talk a little bit about his background.

Mr. Waters, who brought Mrs. Waters for the reception, told William that he had left Mississippi in 1943, after he had been discovered and recorded by the famous folklorist Allen Lomax. Before that, he told us, "I was choppin' cotton, pickin' cotton, drivin' a tractor, doing anything you're supposed to be doing on a plantation.

51

"I got started [singing the blues] when I was a kid. When I was three years old I used to get me little tin cans and things and beat on them and get me a sound going. And then when I was like six or seven years old I had one of those jew's harps. After that I picked up the harmonica, the french harp. I found out how to do something with the bottleneck and *boom!* Out went the harp—in come the guitar!

". . . We didn't have anything to do back in the older days but go home and get together and find a guitar and get some enjoyment going for ourselves, you know. When you work five or six days to go to the city, you can't stay out very long. Rainy days we'd get together and we'd be playing harmonica, playing guitar, picking up pecans, shooting dice for the pecans. We just had a ball."

John Alexander is a Mississippi-born opera star, who has been one of the leading tenors of the Metropolitan Opera for some twenty years. William first met him many years ago at a conference for teen-agers at Belhaven College, and he still remembers John Alexander singing "Jeanie with the Light Brown Hair."

We were very pleased to have a chance to have a dinner for John when he was in Jackson in connection with the operatic program at Millsaps College. He was reared at Meridian. Two of his sisters, who still live in Mississippi, were among our guests that night.

After the dinner John talked about his own career, and the possibilities for other Mississippians having careers in classical music. He believes that with both talent and hard work, it is still very much possible. In John's case, the dedication of his mother to the operatic goal was probably the greatest influence.

The John Alexander story that I liked the most, though, was about a dinner in a New York restaurant. It was a place where some of the Metropolitan artists liked to dine informally and talk shop.

One night at such a dinner a birthday cake was brought to a lady at the next table. Neither John nor any of the other singers knew the lady, but they spontaneously rose and sang "Happy Birthday" with the finest operatic flourishes.

The startled honoree for this attention applauded and said, "Oh, you all should be singing at the Met!"

Among creative artists, William's favorites are the writers, primarily because he is a great reader, as well as something of a writer himself.

We had a lovely evening with Elizabeth Spencer, a native of Canallton, Mississippi and a graduate of Bilhaven College, a small presbyterian College in Jackson, who has long been identified as one of the best active novelists and short story writers—recognition which began with her novels, *Fire in the Morning, Voice at the Back Door* and *Light in the Piazza.*

I first knew Elizabeth when she taught at Northwest Mississippi Junior College in my hometown of Senatobia. She was awarded a Guggenheim fellowship for study and writing in Italy more than twenty years ago. In Italy she married an Englishman, John Rusher, who has taken her to live in Canada, but when she came to the Mansion in the summer of 1981, she still sounded as though she had just left Carrollton the week before.

She seems to be an intensely shy person, and she had no prepared speech for the after-dinner gathering that evening. The questions and the discussions were in good part about the mechanics of actual writing, including the very broad one, "Just how do you sit down and write a novel?" She tried very gamely to answer everything, and I feel sure she enjoyed the give and take, even though she said later, "William, if you had told me just exactly what you expected of me, I really wouldn't have come."

For breakfast the next morning the questions were not so much on the details of writing. There were large groups of faculty and alumni from Belhaven College among the guests (William is a member of the Belhaven Board of Trustees), including several of Elizabeth's classmates and a former roommate. The conversation was easier, but the talk just as intense, and it is likely that more was revealed of Elizabeth Spencer's writing style and concepts here than at the dinner the night before.

One of our most interesting writer guests was Josiah Bunting, a Virginian who had never been in Mississippi before. He is the author of a number of articles in prominent national magazines, but he is perhaps best known for his novel about Vietnam, *The Lionheads*. Mr. Bunting was a company officer in Vietnam, after having been commissioned as first in his class at Virginia Military Institute. Before going to Vietnam, he was a Rhodes Scholar at Oxford, and was later on the history faculty at West Point.

Today Josiah Bunting is president of Hampden-Sydney College at Farmville, Virginia, one of the most distinguished small colleges in the South.

". . .The most serious problem facing higher education in the United States," Dr. Bunting told us, "is the fact that most people don't know what the purpose of education is, any more. Most college presidents and university professors and college teachers have forgotten that their basic mission is to teach people how to express themselves and to be proficient in a profession, and [to try] to get them in the habit of thinking clearly and patiently.

"Many universities, it seems to me, all over the United States have taken on the responsibility of making good the failures of high schools and even primary schools. We always tell our parents at Hampden-Sydney, 'You've had them eighteen years; don't expect miracles in the first two months.'

"We're dealing with eighteen year olds who have had

54

20,000 hours of television when they appear at our campuses, and about 11,000 hours of classroom instruction. The 20,000 hours of television they have had, has been broken up into fourteen-and fifteen-minute chunks interspersed with little *ipilia* of soap ads and worse. What possibilities are there for allowing students to practice Aristotle's dictum that all learning must involve some suffering?"

Mr. Bunting came for a visit at the suggestion of Willie Morris, who was part of what might be called our first "intellectual" evening at the Mansion.

Willie and his good friend, the novelist William Styron, were scheduled to appear together as part of the Millsaps College Arts and Lectures series, and William had invited them to be guests at the Mansion during their visit to Jackson. William Styron came with his wife Rose, and Willie Morris brought his son David. Willie likes to tell that his great-grandfather was introduced to his great-grandmother in the parlor of the Mansion by Governor Henry S. Foote, who happened to be a relative of both Willie Morris and William Winter.

William had been listed on the program to introduce William Styron and Willie Morris, but the discussion after the men spoke became so general that William was as much a part of the panel as they were. In fact, there was some discussion of the changing Mississippi that brought the Governor on an equal panel footing with two well-known novelists. Willie Morris dubbed the panel the "Will, Willie and William Show."

It was very good that we had scheduled a dessert party at the Mansion after the panel at Millsaps. The panel continued in a new setting, broken up only because so many of the guests had to go home to Yazoo City.

At Millsaps, William Styron had read a passage from his (then) new novel *Sophie's Choice*, comparing the American South to Poland. It made a great impression on

William, and he had occasion to read it himself as part of his speech at the celebration of Polish-American Heritage Day at Kosciusko, Mississippi, the next January. Here is that passage:

> Poland is a beautiful, heart-wrenching, soul-split country which in many ways (I came to see through Sophie's eyes and memory that summer, and through my own eyes in later years) resembles or conjures up images of the American South—or at least the South of other, not-so-distant times. It is not alone that forlornly lovely, nostalgic landscape which creates the frequent likeness—the quagmiry but haunting monochrome of the Narew River swampland, for example, with its look and feel of a murky savanna on the Carolina coast, or the Sunday hush on a muddy back street in a village of Galicia, where by only the smallest eyewink of the imagination one might see whisked to a lonesome crossroads hamlet in Arkansas these ramshackle, weather-bleached little houses, crookedly carpentered, set upon shrubless plots of clay where scrawny chickens fuss and peck—but in the spirit of the nation, her indwellingly ravaged and melancholy heart, tormented into its shape like that of the Old South out of adversity, penury and defeat.
>
> Imagine, if you will, a land in which carpetbaggers swarmed not for a decade or so but for millennia and you will come to understand just one aspect of a Poland stomped upon with metronomic tedium and regularity by the French, the Swedes, the Austrians, Prussians, Russians, and possessed by even such greedy incubuses as the Turks. Despoiled and exploited like the South, and like it, a poverty-ridden, agrarian, feudal society, Poland has shared with the Old South one bulwark against its immemorial humiliation, and that is pride. Pride and the recollection of vanished glories. Pride in ancestry and family name, and also, one must remember, in a largely factitious aristocracy, or nobility. The names Radziwill and Ravenel are pronounced with the same intense albeit slightly hollow hauteur. In defeat both Poland and the American South bred a frenzied nationalism. Yet, indeed, even leaving aside these most powerful resemblances, which are very real and

56

which find their origin in similar historical fountains
(there should be added: an entrenched religious
hegemony, authoritarian and puritanical in spirit), one
discovers more superficial yet sparkling cultural cor-
respondences: the passion for horseflesh and military
titles, domination over women (along with a sulky-sly
lechery) a tradition of storytelling, addiction to the
blessings of firewater. And being the butt of mean jokes.

Finally there is a sinister zone of likeness between
Poland and the American South which, although
anything but superficial, causes the two cultures to
blend so perfectly together as to seem almost one in
their shared extravagance—and that has to do with the
matter of race, which in both worlds has produced
centuries-long, all-encompassing nightmare spells of
schizophrenia. In Poland and the South the abiding
presence of race has created at the same instant cruelty
and compassion, bigotry and understanding, enmity
and fellowship, exploitation and sacrifice, searing
hatred and hopeless love. While it may be said that the
darker and uglier of these opposing conditions has
usually carried the day, there must also be recorded in
the name of truth a long chronicle in which decency and
honor were at moments able to controvert the absolute
dominion of the reigning evil, more often than not
against rather large odds, whether in Poznan or Yazoo
City.

The Mansion Inmates

AFTER THE election in November, 1979, I began to think about what would be involved in living in the Governor's Mansion, and how I could best make it a home for my family and for me.

I was aware that through the years inmates from the penitentiary at Parchman had been used for domestic help at the Mansion, even though I was only vaguely familiar with the details of the operation. The use of prison labor was a long-time custom— in Mississippi, as well as many other states—and the cost of changing the system made unlikely any modifications in it. It is an opportunity for some practical job training and, for those who meet the standards, transfer to work release programs and parole.

When we first moved in, there were several men from Parchman who had worked as part of the former Governor's Mansion staff, and they stayed for a few days to help us make the transition.

Then came the five men who were the first to be chosen to come and work with us. For the most part these men were in prison for terrible crimes—most of them for murder. It seemed to me then, and it still does now, to be a strange and unusual qualification for serving here at the Mansion.

I knew their background, and, perhaps because of that, I chose not to go any further than just to learn the names of the men with whom I would be working. But I broke that mental barrier one night, and decided that it was no longer appropriate for me to hide my head in the sand about my staff. It was time that I read their "rap" sheets, and understood the problems of each person.

After I had read their files, it was not a night for easy sleep.

But as the weeks and first months went by, I began to recognize these people as individuals who had made a terrible mistake, but who were obviously trying hard to learn a new skill and who were taking a great deal of pride in their work.

Melba Darras, who had trained many a waiter and waitress at their restaurant in Grenada, took over the job of training them to wait on tables. Neither she nor I realized exactly the type of people we were working with until one day when she told two of the men to take the centerpiece from the main dining room table and put it upstairs on the table in the family quarters.

They thought she meant the center leaf from the table, and proceeded to take it out and bring it upstairs. It was the first time that she and I fully comprehended that this type of work was completely new to these people, and that the learning process had to begin with the most elemental instruction. I think it helped us all to have this rather drastic introduction to our training problems.

Our first large evening affairs were a series of dinners for members of the Legislature and their wives. My first thought was that we would have to hire some experienced help for the first dinner, but Mrs. Darras said, "No, I think these men would really like to try to handle the whole dinner. They are beginning to take a great deal of pride in what they are doing."

That night, as I watched from my end of the long table, I realized that I was a little "uptight" for them —both the waiters and Melba, who was moving about to help and to guide them. I noticed one waiter pouring water with his hand shaking, and pouring wine with a tremble, but I knew they were all doing their best.

I was pleased with their performance, and so were they. I talked to them that night after the dinner, offering both congratulations and praise for the way they had discharged their duties. We had all gone over a hurdle together. Never again was I as nervous or were they as unsure.

In the months since that time, there have been changes among the personnel. Some have gone out on work-release programs, and a few have had to go back to Parchman for a breach of discipline. The ones who are here work with a great sense of pride, and with an understanding that we all work at the total job together.

My first experience in working with prison inmates has led to my developing an increased interest in the overall corrections system. I still have great concern for those persons as individuals, knowing full well that the crimes they have committed are in many instances ghastly, but also well aware, too, that but for the grace of God there go I.

It is natural that from time to time some of the inmates come to me with personal problems related to either their work or their families. It is also a natural reaction for the security officers to feel that this is not appropriate, that I should not be troubled with such matters. I honestly feel that if I were an inmate I could not talk about family problems to a security officer with a gun on his hip.

"Mrs. W. these people aren't here because they were late for Sunday School," the exasperated security men have told me. I realize that, and I think perhaps I am too compassionate on one side and maybe they sometimes tend to be too hard on the other. At any rate, we all work together here, trying to find the middle ground and do a good job.

When one of our first inmate staff (whom I will call Jim) had been with us about six months, the time approached when he would be eligible to go out on work-release program. A requirement for that program is to have a job waiting for you in the "free world," as they say. Jim asked me to help him find a job, and I managed to do that after a few calls. He had made a very good impression on me by not only doing good work on his regular assignments, but by coming to me after he had finished and saying, "I'm through with my jobs, and ready to help you if you need me."

The day Jim left the Mansion to take up his new job we were out of town. We had told him goodbye before we left and wished him good luck, but we did not think about the fact that he was going out without any money into the free world where food and lodging were not free, with the first pay day at least two weeks away. We did not realize this until he came back for a brief visit after a week, a little thinner, but reporting that he had found a co-worker willing to share his lunch.

Jim came back for another visit after that first payday. He was in the kitchen with some of his former colleagues when I came in.

"Mrs. Winter, I have a gift for you," he quickly said, and handed me a crumpled one dollar bill. I shall never forget my momentary agony over whether or not to accept the gift.

Then I realized that it was the most he had to give, and that I certainly did not want to offend him. I took the bill, and still have it in my possession as a reminder of my insensitivity and initial lack of compassion. I shall be forever grateful for having known him.

Forbes Magazine and Chevron

FOR THE people from out of state who have come for our Mansion visits, we have tried to make arrangements to fit their convenience, but when dates have to be set in advance, sometimes months in advance, all sorts of complications may crop up. Take the case of Steve Forbes.

The young president of *Forbes Magazine*, which includes a number of other allied business interests, came with his wife on a Monday afternoon, on what was their first visit to Mississippi. It was obvious that they had come to learn, as much as to talk to us.

Mr. Forbes' office and the headquarters for his magazine, founded by his grandfather, is in New York, but he and Sabrina came to us by way of Washington, to which his father had brought the company yacht for a series of parties planned for officials of the new Reagan administration. On Tuesday he had to be back in New York to be host for the Japanese ambassador, who was bringing some Japanese businessmen that the State Department thought it important for him to meet.

To make that luncheon date and some of the preliminary arrangements, Steve and Sabrina had to leave the Mansion at 3 a.m. Some young people might have made a night of it, but they preferred to get a few hours sleep in the Bilbo Room. I let the Mansion security officers, several of whom are always on duty, make the arrangements of getting them to the airport for their flight back to Washington.

The problems are not always merely on the side of the hostess. It seems that in the packing and repacking for Mississippi, Steve Forbes neglected to include a tie that would be suitable for the dinner. William made him a gift of one of his spares, and later received a very handsome replacement.

For the Forbes dinner we had 65 guests, mostly business people and bankers, from over the state. It gave us an opportunity to include a number of friends and supporters who had not yet visited us at the Mansion. This provided a little added flavor for the occasion, which was not the calmest for me.

My problem was an old one for a lot of people—a missing servant in the midst of an important entertainment. One of the housemen, and our prize waiter, had violated the security rules once too often, and as a consequence had to be returned to Parchman at once. Another inmate was brought back to take advantage of the opportunity left by our wayward waiter, but he was obviously not ready to participate in serving the dinner for 65 people. The solution was to hire for the night one of the men who had completed his prison time at the Mansion and was now privately employed in a work program, using the skills he had learned at the Mansion. To take care of the extra-size guest list, we also temporarily hired an additional "graduate" of our Mansion program, and so wound up with a good staff for the night, relieving all my worries.

The Forbes visit was in the spring of 1981, so much of the talk was naturally about the then-freshly unveiled economic program of the Reagan administration—of which both *Forbes Magazine* and Steve Forbes were strong supporters. I was sorry that the main thrust of the conversation was on this Washington issue, for perhaps it prevented an opportunity for Steve to get into a discussion with our local business leaders about their ideas for economic growth in Mississippi.

His advice was not all economic, however. He had some suggestions about good restaurants in New York, at the request of some of his fellow guests, and later sent William a copy of *Forbes'* "year-end review" of New York restaurants. It seems that economic advice often is mixed with advice about good food, so perhaps mixing the affairs of the state along with dinner at the Mansion is not inappropriate.

Another of our visitors whose topic was primarily economic was Kenneth Derr, president of the Chevron Oil Company, and one of the major industrial investors in the future of Mississippi. William had met Ken at a luncheon in San Francisco, the headquarters of Chevron. For his visit to the Mansion he brought along his wife Donna, a very attractive partner, on her first visit to Mississippi.

President Derr gave us the full background of his California company's major involvement in Mississippi—the largest investment of any oil company in our state. Chevron is a part of Standard Oil of California, which built the first major refinery in Mississippi as part of an arrangement with Standard Oil of Kentucky. The Kentucky company was the major gasoline distributor in the Southeast, and it needed a major refinery source in the area.

The arrangement was successful, and the experience of working in Mississippi was so favorable that Mississippi, even though not a major market, was chosen over other possible sites for a vastly larger refinery which Chevron is now building at Pascagoula. As Mr. Derr pointed out, the major purpose of the plant is to refine the lower quality oil which is imported from throughout the world, but in good part from Latin America.

The Pascagoula refinery is Chevron's major interest in Mississippi, but Mr. Derr's company is also interested in oil produced in the state. He thought the trend of lower production in the state, which began some years ago, would continue, but there would be greater utilization of the oil supply still remaining in existing wells, which can be brought out by pumping carbon dioxide down into the ground to help push out the remaining oil (to oversimplify the process.)

Apparently in Mississippi oil which is termed residual (left over from the first extractions from a well) is a major asset in Mississippi that has become more valuable with the worldwide increase in the value of crude oil.

Ken Derr was very frank about the future use of gasoline, especially for a president of one of the world's largest marketers of gas.

"We say that the usage of gasoline in this country will never be as high as it was just two years ago," he replied to a question. "Every year we have a new set of automobiles from Detroit that are more efficient. And because of the increase in price, people are driving less miles."

The cordial atmosphere of the Derr visit to the Mansion will certainly help strengthen the ties of his company with our state. The new Chevron plant at Pascagoula will probably not be in full operation until after William has left the Governorship, but the Mansion visit helped to create further associations with the people and institutions of our state which will obviously be useful when future decisions about expanded facilities are made. In the continuing struggle for recognition of our potential as the site for industrial growth, the added asset of the personal interest and involvement of the Governor of the state is something worth throwing into the competition.

William has visited dozens of industrial and business leaders in New York, Chicago, Los Angeles, Mexico, Europe and Asia, both in regard to specific industry location posibilities and in general introductory expeditions, but he believes that the most effective communication has come when the business leaders come to the state. When these visits include Jackson as part of the itinerary, he always tries to see the visitor either at his office, or at a luncheon at the Mansion, if it is not appropriate to work out a large dinner visit at the Mansion.

Both of us believe that the larger program of Mansion visits makes an important contribution to the knowledge and concept of Mississippi that makes for long range economic progress, but we are also well aware that day-to-day selling has to be done along the way in the process of image building.

Foreign Relations, or the Importance of Onion Rings

IN LINE with William's interest in developing international exposure and contact for Mississippi, two of our early Mansion guests were the Ambassadors to the United States from Mexico and China. They were sharply different kinds of persons. Ambassador Hugo Margain of Mexico is a scholar-diplomat, well versed about the United States and our economic and political affairs. Ambassador Chai Zemin, from the People's Republic of China, is a small, reserved man, making a quest for knowledge about the United States in his role to help chart the first official relations between the two countries.

Ambassador Chai spoke no English, and all conversation was through his official interpreter, but he could carry on a detailed discourse through that system, a difficult process to follow unless one is accustomed to the "echo" of a running translation.

The Ambassador was with us right after the 1980 Presidential campaign. When Speaker of the House Buddie Newman asked him what he thought of candidates Carter and Reagan, Mr. Chai first replied with a question:

"Are you a Democrat or a Republican?"

When the Speaker admitted to being a Democrat, Ambassador Chai cast his reply in the traditional neutrality of the official foreigner, but perhaps it was diplomatically shaded to meet the obvious preferences of the people at the table.

What I remember most about the meals served the Chinese party, however, was the more private breakfast that followed his second night with us, after the official dinner and breakfast.

Ambassador Chai had asked to visit several representative areas of Mississippi, and we asked him to stay over for a night at the Mansion for this purpose. On the second evening, the local people who were acting as hosts for his Mississippi acclimatization took him to a popular catfish restaurant in the Jackson area.

I learned about this when the Ambassador came down to breakfast the next morning.

Mr. Chai brought down a helping of fried onion rings, in a little paper sack, and he ate them along with his regular breakfast. It seems that the restaurant onion rings had so attracted him the night before that he had asked for a portion to take away. Tommie Darras was horrified to learn that someone has had to supplement his very special breakfast with stale onion rings not even warmed over—he would have been glad to have prepared some fresh ones.

But we really could not take exception to our guest's taste. He was so very polite in his explanation, just as he was about everything else. If onion rings turn up as a new staple in China, a Mississippi catfish restaurant can take the credit.

William could find no way to identify Mississippi as a possible exporter of onions, but he, along with people from our Department of Economic Development, and a number of bankers and industrialists over the state, talked about a myriad of possible business connections. I learned that cotton and soybeans are major items among U.S. exports to China, and that there are prospects of increasing Mississippi's share of these sales.

"China is committed to developing Sino-U.S. relations because this conforms to both our best interests, and is popular among our people," Ambassador Chai told us. "China is now readjusting its economy. Our top priority is the development of light industry both to create funds and meet the material needs of our people."

Both Mr. Chai and the other members of his party stressed the importance of increasing domestic food production in China, as well as the continuing need for them to import agricultural products.

"We have a saying in China," the Ambassador said. "It is good to have more people if you are faced with an enormous job, but it is better to have fewer people if there is little food."

One of the highlights of the dinner for the Chinese guests was the presence of an experienced traveler to China from Mississippi. Mayor Unita Blackwell, of Mayersville, first went to China as a member of a special women's group led by the movie actress Shirley Maclaine. Mrs. Blackwell has been back several times since then.

Ambassador Chai told us that he believed the mayor had been to a number of places in China that he had never seen himself.

China is the largest country in the world, but Mexico is the closest large country to Mississippi, and William believes that it has an important potential market for Mississippi products. Mexico City, he predicts, will probably be the largest city in the world by the end of this century.

"This is a new approach, and I am pleased to be part of it," Ambassador Margain said, in reply to specific questions about how industry in Mississippi could bear up to the production of products likely to be in demand in Mexico as a result of the increased oil production there.

"We have been good friends too long for us to let temporary problems interfere with the economic goals which can be beneficial to both our countries and to your state," was his answer to another question about a specific trade problem.

As a direct result of the Margain visit, William made a trade-seeking trip to Mexico a few months later, and efforts that will produce results both directly and indirectly are still underway.

Mrs. Margain told me about some of her experiences as a hostess in Washington. I discovered that we sometimes had similar problems, but certainly none of mine came from this very attractive lady, who knew how to be a perfect guest.

William's interest in foreign affairs has resulted in the Southern Center for International Studies, which is located in Atlanta, asking his support in regard to official foreign missions and visitors in our country. He has attended some of these meetings in Atlanta and other cities, and has also brought a number of visitors to the Mansion and to his office as part of his work. Sometimes it has not been appropriate to publicize such meetings, but I am sure that they have helped make Mississippi a better known place abroad.

Turner Catledge

FOR THE Mansion visit of Turner Catledge, the Mississippian who became the long-time managing editor of *The New York Times* after being one of the nation's top political reporters, we invited a large number of people from Neshoba and Choctaw counties, many of them part of the Turner and Catledge families. Most of them drove over late in the afternoon, and back home that night. This kind of attendance perhaps increased the anecdotal nature of the visit, for it gave Mr. Catledge the chance to tell dozens of stories about his Mississippi background, and about both Mississippi and national politicians.

The stories told a lot about Mississippi and the nation, and the changes possible in one lifetime, but they also told a lot about the changes in Mississippi from one social event at the Mansion to another. Mr. Catledge told how, as a young boy he had come to Jackson to see President William Howard Taft, who was in Jackson to address the Mississippi State Fair.

"Coming down from Philadelphia took us all day long," Mr. Catledge said. "We had to go to Newton and change trains, and come on over here. It took most all of one day and you'd have to stay overnight; you couldn't go back.

"We had a horse-drawn parade; we didn't trust automobiles then in parades, even in funerals. So it was a horse-drawn parade up Capitol Street. [I suppose] I was looking for a king with a fleece, because my father had told me that a president was something like a king. I was looking for a king with a fleece-lined velvet robe, scarlet,

71

of course, with a crown on his head, a scepter in his hand.

" 'Where is the President?' I asked.

' "There he is, that big fat man there,' my father answered. And he later told the story many times: that after I got down from the window from which I had watched the parade, I said 'Shucks, he's just a man.' "

Mr. Catledge then told how his father had taken him to the Mansion grounds, where Governor Edmond Noel was the host at a garden reception for the President.

"I was just standing around, I didn't have any interest in the President at all," Mr, Catledge continued. "He let me down—just 340 pounds of disappointment. But Senator Anse McLaurin came over and grabbed me by the hand to take me to the President. I pulled back. I wouldn't go.

"I'm sure, in perfect honesty, that [my refusal to meet the President] was the reaction of a shy kid, but there was something about that man that I didn't like. One thing, his appearance disappointed me. Another thing, I'm sure I had this in my bones, because I got this almost with my mother's milk: I didn't like Republicans."

Turner Catledge didn't meet William Howard Taft in the garden of the Mississippi Governor's Mansion, but he was later to know personally and well all the presidents from Herbert Hoover on. He knew and appreciated Hoover from the time when the then-Secretary of Commerce visited the lower Mississippi Valley to inspect the 1927 flood damages. His greatest fame as a newspaper reporter came while participating in Franklin Roosevelt's "around the desk" press conferences, as the correspondent for *The Baltimore Sun* and *The New York Times;* but his later experiences included singing hymns at the National Press Club, accompanied at the piano by Richard Nixon, and knowing the various presidential views on world and national issues through their confidential editorial conferences with the *Times.*

The *Neshoba Democrat* was the first newspaper Mr.

Catledge worked for in Mississippi, and he went from there across to the Delta and the *Tunica Times*, from which he graduated to the *Memphis Commercial Appeal*, where all the top reporters were working on the great flood of 1927. When Secretary Hoover came down to coordinate Red Cross relief [there were no government funds in 1927, but in 1928 a federal flood control program was passed], he asked the editor of the *Commercial Appeal* to let him talk to a reporter who had been out in the field covering the flood. After young Catledge's long report to Mr. Hoover in his suite at the Peabody Hotel, the Secretary asked the editor to let Catledge be assigned to him as a special assistant for the rest of his stay in the flood zone.

"While [Mr. Hoover) was in the office car of his special train in the railroad yards in New Orleans, he wrote a letter to Mr. Adolph Ochs, publisher of *The New York Times*, saying, 'You asked me to be on the lookout for talent for your paper. I've found a young man named Turner Catledge that you ought to look into.' "

To paraphrase Mr. Catledge's story, Publisher Ochs sent the letter from Hoover along to his managing editor. The managing editor did what managing editors do with such requests from publishers—he filed it in a bottom drawer.

Not long after that, Mr. Catledge went to work for *The Baltimore Sun*, and was one of their Washington reporters. Here he met Herbert Hoover again, when he covered a White House press conference—by now, *President* Hoover. Not long after that, Adolph Ochs was a luncheon guest of the President.

"I wrote you once about a young man, and I never heard from you!" he told the publisher. "I saw him here yesterday. He was at a press conference. He's now with *The Baltimore Sun.*"

To let Mr. Catledge take up the story: "When Ochs got back to his office, he called in his managing editor and said, 'What did you do with this letter I sent you?" The editor didn't remember any letter about Turner Catledge, but he wound up being told, 'Whether you find the letter or not, you get this young man on the paper whatever it takes!'

"Now believe me, had I known about that letter, I'd have gotten more than the $75 a week I got! But, I tell you, things have a way of working out. Things worked out very well. I have no complaints."

Mr. Catledge was asked the inevitable question about why there seem to be so many native Mississippians who are so prominent in literature and journalism.

"Best answer I ever heard was from George Allen, the White House funny man who came up from Okolona. He said 'Well, it's better work than plowing.'

"I've never found a Southern accent to be any hindrance at all," Catledge added. "Quite the contrary. Because you usually find that in any group, you'll find another Southerner in the same fix with you. And especially when you run into Mississippians—they've got to stick together or find themselves getting stuck separately."

Mr. Catledge expressed his great respect for President Hoover, but said that Franklin D. Roosevelt was the most impressive of the famous public figures with whom he had been associated in his long years at the top of the newspaper profession. But, he added,

"I think Harry Truman was one of the four greatest Presidents we ever had. He faced more critical problems during his years as President than almost any other four Presidents combined. He pulled them off quite well."

Iris Kelso, a well-known newspaper woman in New Orleans, is a native of Philadelphia, Mississippi, and happens to be a cousin of Turner Catledge. We invited her to share his visit, and her comments in her column in the *Times-Picayune* are worth quoting here:

> The after-dinner conversation was rich . . . Like many Southerners, Catledge is an accomplished story-teller. Sitting there in this exquisite parlor, where every piece

Elise Winter, Eudora Welty

The Winters greet President Jimmy Carter—Oct. 31, 1980

The Mississippi Governor's Mansion

Mrs. Anne Winter Williams, Lele Winter, William Winter, Elise Winter, Eleanor Winter

Mrs. Joel Varner serving at Reception

President Carter with the Winter family

Ted Turner, William Winter

At the Inauguration

Muddy Waters, William Winter

Bill Ferris, Leontyne Price, William Winter, Eudora Welty, Willie Morris

Elizabeth Spencer, William Winter

Senator John Stennis, Elise and William Winter, Senator Sam Nunn

Lillian Carter, Elise Winter

Four generations—Mrs. Milton Cushman, Mathew Cushman,
Mrs. E. W. Varner, Mrs. J. T. Phillips

At the Mondale visit

Dean Rusk

Eudora Welty, Edward Stasheff,
Margaret Walker Alexander

A Reception Line in the Rain

Tea for Shirley Hufstedler, Secretary of Education

Ambassador Chai Zemin *Emory Cunningham*

Phineas Stevens, Harold Burson, Fred Nelson, Harold Gotthelf,
William Winter

William Winter and Ambassador Hugo Margain

Tandy Rice, William Winter, Jerry Clower

Eudora Welty, William Winter, Walker Percy

William Winter, Eudora Welty, Leontyne Price, Elise Winter

Melba Darras

Mississippi's No. 1 Jogger

Tommie Darras

Bill Clinton, William Winter, David Bowen, Sonny Montgomery

William Winter and Nicky

of furniture is a museum piece, we heard Catledge's intimate recollections of a 50-year period of American history. The audience ranged in age from men and women who remembered that day during the Depression when the banks failed, to young people who only vaguely remembered John Kennedy as President. They had seen him on television as children. Several of the younger guests were black, members of Winter's staff and their friends.

Afterward, I went up to my room—the biggest bedroom I have ever seen. A plate of fruit, a dish of mints and a silver pitcher of ice water were on the antique table by the bed.

When Mrs. Winter took me in the room, she told me this was the Leontyne Price bedroom, named after the opera star from Laurel, Mississippi, who was a guest of the Winters for his inauguration in January.

Mrs. Winter made no big thing of it. This was the Leontyne Price bedroom just as Catledge's was the Theodore Bilbo bedroom, named after the race-baiting Mississippi governor and U.S. Senator who is a part of Mississippi's past.

During the visit, Catledge said, "It's wonderful to be here with home folks!" Mississippi, like Louisiana, has a special hold on its people. For me, going home to spend a night at the Governor's Mansion, to key into a state that is still in the midst of tremendous change, was a moving reminder of where my heart remains.

Walker Percy

OUR DINNER for Walker Percy was in June of 1981. I remember that the rose garden on the Mansion grounds was not producing very well, and I had to ask friends for help. Roses came in from all around town, and there were enough for flower arrangements in the bedrooms and hallways upstairs.

We needed the extra flowers, because in addition to Dr. Walker Percy and his wife, we had his brother LeRoy and his wife Sarah, along with their son Billy and his wife from Greenville. The next morning I learned that Walker's wife, Bunt, was also very much interested in flowers. She joined me in the garden shortly after 6:30, and we had a fine time cutting roses and picking a few nasturtiums to add to the breakfast arrangements. Bunt is from Doddsville, and she learned her flowers there long before she and Walker settled in Covington, Louisiana.

But perhaps what I remember most about the Walker Percy visit was his response to the question, "Why does Mississippi produce so many writers?"

It is a question that William and I have heard all over the country, and one that always seems to come up at the Mansion entertainments for writers. Walker Percy was obviously a little bored with the question:

"Mississippi? That's the question everybody has always asked and I've never heard a good answer," he said. "I think the answer has to be individual. With me it was just a case of being lucky, of being exposed to my uncle who was a wonderful man, a wonderful writer . . . I think he affected a great many people in Greenville. I think at one time somebody told me Greenville had fifty-four published writers. I think a great many of them were traceable to him.

"I think that's true maybe all over the state, people like Eudora Welty and Faulkner. I don't know why Mississippi rather than Ohio or North Carolina. The classical answer is that in the South and particularly in the rural South there is a greater sense of community, a greater sense of place, a family tradition that makes good novels. Maybe so. I don't know."

Both at dinner and at breakfast that morning Percy had a lot of questions about the influences on his writing, his procedure and the actual background to his becoming a writer. From my journal, and from a recording of some of his discussion, I think the chapter on his and Bunt's visit can best be told largely through excerpts from his comments.

". . . it's strange how these things come about. It was purely by accident that I'm here. It was an accident that I became a writer. I set out to become a doctor. I took an M.D. degree. I picked up a bug and got sick and during my convalescence I had an opportunity to read. I read for a year and half or two years which I hadn't had a chance to do going to pre-med school before.

"Actually I was doing autopsies in the TB divison of Bellevue Hospital in New York. I did over 100 and I just picked up a case of tuberculosis. Fortunately it wasn't very serious. But it was enough. In those days you had to go to a sanitorium. It was enough so that you were flat on your back for a couple of years with nothing to do but read. Actually, to tell you the truth, I was the happiest man ever to get out of medicine.

"I was delighted because I had always secretly wanted to be a writer in the South, although I should have known better. I know a couple of respectable people who have become writers. But I had also lived, with my two brothers, with William Alexander Percy for 10 or 15 years, and being exposed to him in itself was enough to get you excited about writing."

Dr. Percy reported that his first writing experience had been for the Greenville High School paper, the *Pica*, where he wrote the gossip column called "The Man in the Moon," and kept up with who was dating whom.

"We had a wonderful English teacher named Mrs. Hawkins, who made us write sonnets. I got pretty good doing that. I would write a sonnet in half an hour. It wasn't very good, but it rhymed and had the right meter and so forth. I got so I could sell them. I'd sell them for fifty cents, and did very well.

"I can remember the first time I ever wanted to be a writer. I remember (most of you don't), there was a magazine called *Liberty* which cost a nickel. They had something called the short, short story. If you could write a short, short story which could fit in on one page, they would pay, oh, I don't know, $500. I tried that at age 12, 13, and 14, and no sale."

But he did describe his first published writing (other than for the *Greenville Pica*, after describing the influences of other writing.

"I guess I didn't get a good education. I didn't get a chance to take much literature; I took very little English. I still haven't read an English novel, which is a terrible thing to say. I wasn't interested in Mr. Faulkner even though he was almost next door. He used to come play tennis with my uncle, which meant nothing to me. But being flat on my back for two years I read and read.

". . . I think everybody comes at writing in different ways. For me it wasn't the particular American or Southern tradition. I came about through Russian novels and French novels. I remember I read a book by an author named Suzanne Langer . . . a very exciting book with some things I liked and some things I didn't. (Incidentally, it's when you don't like something that usually the best things happen; you get excited or provoked.) So I wrote a review for Suzanne Langer's book and sent it off to a magazine called *Thought,* and, lo and behold, it was published. I couldn't believe it. Of course all I got paid was reprints. I got about 100 reprints.

"It was nice getting published. I wrote several reviews on philosophy and book reviews on psychiatry, getting paid with reprints. I decided, having read the French writers, particularly Proust and Sartre, that the French have something we don't have. They have the position which is not so strong here of getting excited about ideas, philosophy and theology. And strangely it came into fiction which usually here is compartmented—you do one thing or the other.

"So I thought, well, why not try writing a book which illustrated some of the things I was thinking about. I was thinking about religion and distance and predicament and so forth. I wrote two extremely bad novels, and unless you were a genius you couldn't get through them, and thank God they haven't been published. But I think it's necessary to do that. Then one day I just . . . there's this funny kind of dialectic between getting up and saying well, 'it's hopeless,' you can't do it, forget it, but then having done that, having said it's hopeless then somehow or another you have nothing to lose so you say, 'oh well, rather than jumping in the river why not just write a couple of sentences?'

"Then I wrote *The Moviegoer* in which somehow or other, as the critics say, I found a voice, I found a way of saying something which suited me. That was pretty good, I thought, that you could write what you wanted to, when you wanted and also translate into fiction ideas you were thinking about. It happened to work. It was a good thing. As I said, I think all writers come at fiction from different angles."

There were several questions about the influence and

the relationship of his education as a doctor of medicine on his writing.

"I think my medical background might have had some bearing on [the theme of my writing] because the main stance of a doctor is diagnostic. He's faced with pathology, somebody with something wrong with him. Maybe I sort of picked that stance up. I began to approach it from the modern man as a man-in-a-predicament, from a diagnostic point of view. I wrote about it from the point of view of what's wrong with him.

"I guess what distinguished me from most other Southern writers is that I was not particularly interested in the things that make Southern writing particularly the best, the idea of a strong sense of time and place and rootedness and the family. All that is very admirable, but I was more interested in what happens to a man or a woman who has moved from the admirable Southern village and finds himself in Atlanta or New Orleans or heartbroke in New Orleans or a retired millionaire in Grandfather Mountain, North Carolina . . . what's that like? So that is really what I've been doing . . .

"Yeah, it [the discipline of medical school] really did [influence me] although you might think it's a strange preparation—education—for a writer, to go to medical school for four years and then be an intern. For one thing, a rather superficial thing, I had just enough knowledge of psychiatry that I could create my own syndromes. There's not enough known about psychiatry that anybody could dispute me. It's funny, in this last book (*The Second Coming*) I made up a whole different disease. I called it Houseman's Syndrome, characterized by falling down . . . this guy falls down in bunkers on the golf course occasionally . . . instead of having amnesia he remembers everything, everything that ever happened to him . . . I made up a whole list of things and called it Houseman's Syndrome.

"I got letters from three neurologists who told me that there was such a thing. It was called temporal lobe epilepsy. And sure enough, there was no cure for it. I also made up a cure in there (the book) but I don't think it worked. The fellow kept falling down even at the end.

"I think the world is in so much trouble now that the whole attitude of the novelist is one of examination and diagnosis of what's wrong with the world, what's going wrong. So I think a medical stance, a psychiatric stance toward a nutty world, is not inappropriate for a novelist."

There were questions related to several topics of the day. One was about how the term "humanism" had become suspicious and quite often a word of disapprobation.

"I think it has fallen into disrepute because it's used in the phrase 'secular humanism,' which is kind of a real putdown. I accept the description of Christian humanism, at least as it applies to fiction, because, for me at least, Christian theology fits very well with the vocation of the novelist. I think, after all, the novel is about something going on in a real world, about a man in trouble, a woman in trouble, about a pilgrim of sorts, some quest of sorts, going toward a destination of sorts.

"Of course this is the very climate of Christian theology. You've got a man who is a wayfarer, a pilgrim on a quest in search of something. To me it's the natural background for my fiction. So much so that I can't imagine being a good Buddhist or being a good Marxist and writing novels . . . I've noticed very few good novelists come out of Freudianism, Marxism or Buddhism."

Walker's visit was shortly after the immense publicity for the novel *Confederacy of Dunces*, so he was asked to recount the story of how he had gotten it published, after it had been ignored for many years after the author's suicide.

"Well, [the story] was sad. I wish I could say that I knew what was going to happen with that novel but I didn't.

What happened was that (in the process of teaching a course on creative writing) I read 200 bad novels in order to find one that was pretty good.

"As the course started I began to get calls from this strange lady who said that she had this great novel I had to read, written by her son. Her son had been dead twelve years, suicide. The last thing I wanted to do was to read it. But she was such a pest, she persisted so much. She came in and just dumped it on my desk. It was a mess. It looked like about the sixth or seventh carbon, a smeared carbon copy. Usually I got so good at reading all this stuff that I could read a page or even a paragraph and tell it was no good. I thought I could get off the hook by reading a couple of pages and know it was no good and be able to tell the lady that I did my best.

"The fact was, it *was* good. It was very good. I sent it to my own publisher and he was not interested. It had been the rounds of about ten or twelve publishers while [the author] was alive. His mother blames her son's suicide on the fact that it was rejected by Simon and Schuster. I finally sent it to LSU—a new editor. He said, 'I think you're right; I think it's good, I think we'll publish it. We're going to lose money, but the most we can expect to lose is $5,000. It'll take $10,000 to publish 2,000 copies. We'll stand to lose $5,000, but I think I can get a federal grant to cut the loss to $2,000.' So he got the federal grant.

"Then strange things began to happen. Even before the first edition was published, it was sold out. It got a couple of rave reviews in *Publisher's Weekly* and other early reviews. We were delighted to sell the paperback rights for $2,000. I thought maybe the best that could be expected of it was that it would be a popular local book. Maybe a sort of semi-classic about New Orleans. Very remarkable delineation of New Orleans types. But that was all. I can't account for it . . . why people in Des Moines, or Seattle or New York can understand it so well or like it so much."

Someone asked:

"Did Mrs. Toole [the author's mother] have the grace not to gloat?"

"No," Walker answered, "she's gloating all over the place."

But the recurring theme of the guests' discussion with the author was the Mississippi experience and the Southern experience. William recalled Walker's foreword to a new edition of *Lanterns on the Levee*, and asked,

"What would Will Percy think about where we are now?"

"I think I asked that same question in the introduction," Walker said. "I wondered what he would think. He would be astounded. He knew all about Bilbo. He knew nothing about William Winter. He would not find it credible that this could be happening. I don't think that anybody could have foreseen the changes that have occurred since his death in 1942. I don't think he would have."

"You could certainly predict," William replied, "that he would have been in the forefront of the moderate progressive leadership that has enabled us to make this transition, couldn't you?"

"I think so, yes. He got blamed for being a paternalistic segregationist, but it's easy to look back in hindsight. Most white people in the 1930's were the same way, and yet he was known as a wild-eyed radical in Greenville, and much too liberal.

"I was asking the Governor a while back, has any society seen such a change in one generation? I can only say that it makes you feel extremely hopeful. The difference between the politics in Mississippi when I left in 1946, and politics in Mississippi now—it's a tremendously hopeful thing to see.

"I don't feel the same way about the future of Southern writing. Somebody was asking, who's good among young Southern writers? I always have trouble thinking of somebody. There are not many. I read an article yesterday called "The Demise of Southern Literature," the usual thesis that what has happened with the South is that the South has been homogenized, simply been taken over, the interstates, the shopping centers, it's just like the North and that's the end of Southern literature. I don't think that's really true. I think that we're still different in spite of everything. Atlanta may be one of the most urbanite places in the country, but you know you're in the South and nowhere else. So is Jackson."

William, who went to college a few years later than Dr. Percy, was aware of the strong standing of the University of North Carolina during that period, so he asked about the influence of Chapel Hill. Interestingly enough, Percy had written a piece for *Carolina* magazine about movie-going.

"I wasn't much aware of [a special atmosphere for Chapel Hill]," Percy continued. "It's amazing how little you are aware of things when you were in college. Talk about dumb, I was there right in the middle of all the terrible strikes, almost a revolution, of the cotton mill workers around Gastonia. There was W.J. Cash writing a remarkable book down in Charlotte. All of this was going on and what were we doing? We were sitting on the front porch of the SAE house.

"Now that I think about it, one thing that happened was very important. When I was a sophomore, Douglas Southall Freeman's *R.E. Lee* was taught us—four volumes—I remember reading that—an extraordinary experience. I remember reading *Look Homeward Angel.* Thomas Wolfe had just written that a few years earlier, and I *saw* Thomas Wolfe walking down the steps of the library. He was like a mythical figure; he looked like he was eight feet tall."

"I wondered about Wolfe, whether you had known him," William commented.

"I didn't know him, but I *saw* him," Walker replied.

There were questions about Dr. Percy's writing habits, and that brought about a discussion into which another guest, Eudora Welty entered.

Question—How do you get yourself up for writing?

"You don't," Dr. Percy answered. "I mean you start out at 9:00 in the morning whether you feel bad or not. You don't keep yourself up. What you do is sit there. You give yourself no choice. You sit there. The funny thing is that sometimes the worst mornings, like a bad Monday morning, you get up and the last thing in the world you want to do is to sit there and on the worst mornings sometimes the best things happen. Right, Eudora?"

Welty: "Um hmm."

Percy: "Sometimes you feel like everything is going good, then it's no good."

Welty: "Especially if you look forward for so long, you're going to have a wonderful, uninterrupted time next Tuesday. Then when you wake up on Tuesday and it's uninterrupted and you're paralyzed. Whereas if you had a hard time and everything interrupted you all day, you could probably do something. It's not fair. Not that it's ever meant to be fair."

Percy: "I'll tell you what's unfair about it. I think you enjoy your work more than I do. I don't really. For me it's a pain."

Welty: "I love it."

Percy: "I know you do. You ruin everything for the stereotype of the way writers are supposed to be. You *like* to write. You are not alienated. You stay here in Jackson all through the summer. You ought to be up in Martha's Vineyard with Bill Styron."

I doubt if the parlor of the Governor's Mansion had ever before been the setting for a discussion of the pangs of literary production by two of the world's foremost practitioners of the art. But here we were, and we loved it.

Home Cooking

THE GOVERNOR'S Mansion is divided into two distinct areas—the historic part at the front, with four large bedrooms upstairs and dining rooms and parlors downstairs, and the relatively new annex built at the rear of the house.

The first annex was built by Governor and Mrs. Edmond Noel around 1908, as part of a remodeling. When a general reconstruction was carried out in the administration of Governor Waller in the early 1970's, almost all of the entire rear annex was taken down and replaced.

Our private living quarters are upstairs in this new annex to the house. This consists of a spacious apartment of four bedrooms, living room, dining room, family room, breakfast room and small kitchen. The kitchen is usually serviced from the main kitchen below by a dumbwaiter.

Even though we have a stove and a refrigerator upstairs, along with the other minimum fixtures, I have found time for very little cooking. After thirty years of marketing, cooking and keeping house, I now have priorities of keeping my own office, going to meetings and making speeches, and running the overall Mansion. There is neither time nor necessity for cooking.

But I do keep my hand in. I have enjoyed cooking too much in the past to give it up. There are several family favorites which I like to think I can still do best, and I prepare them when the notion happens to coincide with the time. One of these is caramel cake, and sometimes cookies that the girls have always liked.

86

All the utensils for cake making haven't been duplicated upstairs, so I usually make the cake in the big kitchen downstairs, and bring it upstairs for baking in the small oven. I never cease to be amazed at the problems of mixing things downstairs, which I only attempt after hours, when the regular cooks are gone. Every utensil—even every cooking spoon and knife, seems to have been made for some jolly green giant, and the canisters for flour, sugar and meal seem to run to ten to fifteen pound sizes. Even the baking powder can seems to be the size of a three pound shortening can.

The icing offers new frustrations in moving the pots and pans back and forth with the dumbwaiter, while I race back and forth to get them. So there is really no great inducement to continue my own cooking, especially when good cooking is a standard part of the Mansion operation.

Sometimes I wonder if I will ever be a good cook again, and if I will ever get back to the near-instinctive preparation of the dishes that we have so much enjoyed as a family. This is an interlude in our lives that I will probably remember as four years without cooking, marketing or cleaning house. Hopefully, my long exposure to the readjustment that comes with politics will make it easy to go back home to the routines of housekeeping and homemaking.

The two full-time women cooks at the Mansion —Lorene Divine and Minnie Miller—came to us after service during several previous administrations. Both are very good cooks, and persons easy to get along with.

They soon found out one of William Winter's favorite things in life is pecan pie, and that not far behind pecan is coconut custard pie. Now hardly a day goes by without a fresh pecan or coconut pie being made. Of course their repertoire extends to other kinds of pies, but they have learned that pecan and coconut sell better with the governor, and there is always a fresh slice of one, or both, on hand.

My own major sweet-tooth weakness is ice cream, and Melba Darras is a genius at homemade ice cream. Our favorite is the mint ice cream she makes with fresh mint from the garden, and that has become a specialty of the house. She is just about as good with lotus ice cream, lemon and chocolate almond, or just plain vanilla.

The favorite dessert of my daughters is the Mississippi Mud Cake which is made in the downstairs kitchen. When we get letters requesting favorite Mississippi recipes, we usually send the one for Mississippi Mud Cake. The girls also like the cookies made in the shape of the state of Mississippi, which are kept in large tins on the shelf in the kitchen.

This recital of sweet-tooth items may give the impression of an inordinate intake of calories during the current occupation of the Mansion. I am afraid that there would be great excesses along this line if I did not keep up a constant battle with Tommie Darras about those calories.

William's fondness for running, however, more than equals his fondness for pecan pie, so I have no real worries for him, if we can keep a general balance in the meals. Mr. Darras makes a marvelous English trifle that we enjoy in the wintertime, and part of our celebration of spring is the Darras strawberry shortcake. The special Darras dressing for his Greek salad is something that members of his family tell me that nobody else can duplicate, and he can use spices and herbs in marvelous ways to season dozens of other dishes.

The nature of the operation of the Mansion sometimes brings us to a situation where for two or three days in a row there are three "company" meals a day. There comes a time when enough is enough, and we simply have to slow down our eating and get to some plainer foods.

I sometimes think Mr. Darras pretends not to understand:

"What was wrong with that? Why didn't you eat it?"

I think he well knows that there was nothing wrong with the dish—the trouble has been that too many things are too good, and we have to find a way to get down to earth with some ordinary vegetables and plainer fare.

When we are planning for a large dinner, Mr. and Mrs. Darras and I sit down and discuss the menu. Mrs. Darras may have written out two or three possible menus to choose from in their entirety, or we may make selections and changes item by item.

If we are having someone from out of the state, possibly someone who has never been in Mississippi before, we make a special effort to prepare food that is typical of the state—seafood from the coast, or chicken or beef. There is a seafood truck which comes through Jackson every Monday morning, and Mr. Darras makes a purchase every time, varying with the entertainment plans for the week.

The number of guests for lunch or dinner often influences the menu. For thirty or forty people we can serve seafood, maybe trout almondine or some other fish entree very easily, but for one of the larger dinners, beef is better to serve because of the capacity of the stove. Steak can be served immediately as cooked; and for our largest crowds, chicken breasts that can be prepared ahead of time, and still be accommodated by the oven are the surest choice. I have learned a great deal about the various tricks of preparing food for cooking ahead of time, and having the cooking finished just minutes before serving.

When we first came to the Mansion there were problems with the stove—at one time only one of the four eyes on top would burn. One night, for a group of about sixty, we were having filet mignon, and the last steaks were cooking when the stove seemed to collapse, and electricity shorted out. Tommie knew how to coax that last heat in the stove long enough to finish the cooking of the filets. What we would have done had the shutdown come five minutes earlier, I haven't yet dared to think about.

89

We finally managed to budget enough money to buy a replacement for the stove. We got a good bid on a very fine new stove, and we are already saving a lot on repair bills.

I have found that budgeting for the Mansion is considerably different from the old Winter household budget. Instead of struggling to keep my own little account balanced, I have had to operate with a budget prepared more than a year in advance.

In keeping the Mansion budget in balance I have had the invaluable help of Mrs. Margaret Furlow, who is in charge of the whole operating budget for the Governor's office. I jokingly tell Margaret she has to watch the spending closely enough to keep me out of jail, and between us we have instituted a Mansion budget system that has enabled the purchase of essential replacements for silver, crystal and china.

After a year's experience, I had carefully watched the 1981 budget to save a little for some special work after Christmas—planting some trees in parts of the yard, for instance. Then a fiscal crisis brought a freeze on all state expenditures, the Mansion included. Even though the money had been saved previously during the year, we could not spend it. Public budgets are sometimes stricter than household budgets and a little more difficult to understand.

Margaret and I have now established quarterly budgets within the annual total, which makes for more assured planning. We will get the trees planted yet.

A Presidential Political Year

THE OCCUPANTS of the Mississippi Governor's Mansion are chosen through a political process, and so are the occupants of a better known residence at 1600 Pennsylvania Avenue. It was because of that Presidential political process that we had a number of well known and interesting callers in 1980.

We had been in the Mansion only about two weeks when Ethel Kennedy made a visit to Jackson in the interests of her brother-in-law Senator Ted Kennedy. We invited her to breakfast, along with her son, Robert F. Kennedy, Jr., and daughter Courtney.

It was early stages as far as having large numbers of people for breakfast was concerned, and I was by no means sure how the arrangements would go. Despite my concerns about whether everything would be hot and on time, everything went well except for one item which I spotted too late to correct that morning. Perhaps it really was not noticed by anyone else.

We had reached the stage of second cups of coffee when I looked up and realized that the silver coffee pot being used to serve the side of the table opposite Mrs. Kennedy was an old one with no top, and a badly damaged base. My momentary horror was assuaged when I noticed that none of the other guests had their eyes on the second coffee pot. (One of the pots was very nice). That was when I realized that it would be necessary for me to bring my own silver from home. We now have two good silver coffee pots in use, and when we bring in my own silver service we can have the use of four pots. When there are more than sixty people to serve, that many coffee pots are absolutely needed.

Ethel Kennedy has a very warm and vibrant personality, very much as she has been described by the media through the years. She was very much interested when I told her about the time that another one of her brothers-in-law, the then Senator John F. Kennedy, had been a guest in the Mansion when he spoke in Mississippi in 1958.

"I would really like to see the bed that he slept in," Ethel said, "and it won't matter if it is not made up." But I knew without a doubt that it was made up when we went upstairs. The bed in question is what has long been called the Bilbo bed, in the large Victorian style, with a teaster-top. It was given to Theodore G. Bilbo during his first term as Governor by a group of friends and admirers from Vicksburg.

I didn't tell Mrs. Kennedy that a picture of the bed had been used in a later political campaign against J.P. Coleman, who had been John Kennedy's host. John Kennedy was probably the first major political figure to come to Mississippi as part of a presidential nomination campaign. The fact that most of the candidates for both major parties now come to Mississippi is a healthy indication of a better political climate in our state.

Mrs. Joan Mondale, wife of the Vice-President, was another political celebrity who came to the Mansion as part of the campaign for the 1980 Democratic nomination. Mrs. Mondale came to Jackson to dedicate the new federal building down Capitol Street from the Mansion, but she also took the occasion to visit the craft center out on the Natchez Trace Parkway near Ridgeland.

Crafts are not just a contrived media gimmick interest for Joan. At the Natchez Trace Center she examined everything that was being done, and actually "threw a pot" herself. The people at the Craft Center made her a present of a raku teapot which she brought back to the Mansion and pointed out to a number of people in the course of a reception which we gave for her.

Later that year we were in Washington, and attended a reception given by Vice-President and Mrs. Mondale at their official residence. There, prominently displayed on one of the coffee tables, was the raku teapot. Joan made a point to show it to me, and there is no doubt in my mind that the small gift made an indelible impression of Mississippi for this very gracious, and very craft-conscious lady.

A number of other prominent visitors and celebrities came to the Mansion during the campaign year—people ranging from cabinet officers to star athletes like Hank Aaron. But undoubtedly the most colorful one of the celebrities was Mrs. Lillian Carter, the President's mother.

There was no trouble packing the Mansion for a reception in her honor, after she had gone to a local high school for a visit with students that made a good televised media event. It was part of a carefully programmed campaign schedule, but she sounded very much like a good Southern mother when she spoke to us from a perch halfway up the staircase.

"I never thought Jimmy would be President of the United States, but I want all of you to vote for him," was her very direct message.

She had to be whisked away for another engagement, but not before she had a chance to speak to some old friends, most of whom predated her son's prominence as Governor and President. These included Dr. Dick Yelverton, of Jackson, who had been a member of the fraternity during the time she served as house mother at the Kappa Alpha house at Auburn.

"Well, Dickie, I didn't think anything good would ever come of you and here you are a doctor," she teased him in front of everybody. But it was obvious she was teasing, and Dr. Yelverton didn't mind.

It was only a week or two after Miss Lillian's visit to Jackson that she fell and broke her hip, thus ending her campaign stint.

William strongly feels that now that Mississippi has become a campaign stop for all candidates of both parties, the political leadership of the state should take an active role in the national campaigns. We campaigned actively for President Carter as the Democratic nominee, and we were highly pleased when we learned that he was going to make a visit to Jackson as part of his last campaign swing just a few days before the election.

The news about President Carter's visit brought a rush of preparations to the Mansion, and it also brought an awareness of some of the inconveniences of Presidential security. The personal security arrangements for the Governor and his family have brought a certain inconvenience to us, but the adaptation had worked so smoothly that we very rarely noticed them after the first few weeks.

The Governor's security is in charge of a special detail chosen from the Mississippi Highway Safety Patrol—fine looking young men who blend into the background at the Mansion, and become a part of the every day way of life. They operate on a round-the-clock schedule, admitting visitors to the Mansion, accompanying William wherever he goes (a security man needs to be a good jogger) and serving as very unobtrusive escorts to me when I travel or meet engagements over the state. The security men are a necessary part of the staff of the Govenor's office and the Mansion, and they accept a quiet but efficient role as part of William's team.

My first real introduction to the Mansion security system came on our first night spent in the Governor's bedroom. The canopied bed heightens the darkness of the whole large room, but the little lights from the bedside telephone which come on when a line is in use literally light up the room like a flashlight within a tent.

I was startled from time to time in the night by the recurring lights, but saved from being fully awakened by a ringing telephone. I began to learn how helpful the screening process maintained for the Governor by the State Highway Patrol really is. When those lights flashed on into the wee hours, calls were coming in, but the callers were being answered by the security staff people on duty. Individual buzzers ring the various extensions.

The system is by no means as elaborate as at a place like the White House, for instance, but it serves a very helpful purpose for the Governor of Mississippi. He doesn't have to be awakened unless there is a real emergency.

Answering the phone is no simple telephone operator-type task. There is the inevitable problem of some person who has had too much to drink, and then calls back repeatedly after being turned off the first time. There are sometimes unstable persons who seem to have no idea of the time of night. The Governor is interested in what any citizen has to say about what he has done or not done, but not in the middle of the night.

The security staff is constantly on the alert for any physical threats against the Governor or members of his family, and through it all these young men remain calm and collected. I have the greatest admiration for these men who do a difficult job so well. Some of those who work for us at the Mansion have done the same job for several other Governors, and others have come into the job as we go along. They are professionals in the best sense of the word.

When there is any kind of function at the Mansion the security staff is on duty at the point of entrance, opening the door and helping us to greet the guests. Sometimes the security man has the job of counting the guests. Usually this is to make sure that all the invited ones have arrived, but sometimes it is to make sure that there are no gate-crashers, accidental or otherwise.

The front gates to the Mansion, opening on the sidewalk of Capitol Street, are very rarely opened, because of the problem of uncontrolled entrance. We like to have them open for evening functions, for parking is often available on the street, and it is limited inside the grounds. Sometimes people come in from the street on these occasions. If the affair is a reception-type event, the trespass is usually ignored and the interposing individual welcomed in with the rest of the crowd. If it is a limited invitation event, such as our dinners, with seating spaces reserved, the security people have the job of gently discouraging those who have not been invited.

When I travel over the state as a representative of the Governor at some official function, to make a speech or to cut a ribbon, a security person travels with me, to help with travel arrangements and to be sure that I arrive safely and at the right place and time. Moving about Jackson for routine unofficial tasks and visits—department store, beauty parlor, a friend's house—I feel no need for a security escort.

I think the greatest service the security men provide for me personally is when they call in, sometimes through a radio relay, to report that William has arrived safely at his destination. The constantly tight schedule that he follows in meeting commitments to the people of the state involves a great deal of flying in weather that is not always favorable. I am accustomed to those constant flights, but it is always so very satisfying to have the call and know that he has reached Biloxi, or Booneville, or wherever, safely.

Our security men have some very specific, but firmly enforced rules about security, but most of their operation has been accepted as part of the routine of life at the Mansion, and goes without special notice. I am sure that in the White House some of the same reaction is in evidence, but the President's Secret Service detail makes itself very firmly felt by all who are involved in the arrangements for Presidential travel.

For President Carter's visit, the Secret Service advance detail came to the Mansion a week before the visit, and they had endless questions about everybody's routine. There were some inevitable cross-ups with our own security staff, and I have to admit that I, too, thought some of the people from Washington were at times a little overbearing.

One of the misunderstandings was about the Presidential "hot-line" that has to be with him wherever he goes. They wanted a special line into the Rose Parlor, and it was difficult for me to understand why they could not make an adaptation with the Mansion switchboard, only a few feet away at the side entrance. The Presidential preparations took precedence, however, and before I knew it, there were all sorts of phone lines strung through the trees on the groundsbut not in the Rose Parlor. I presume every care was taken for every contingency, and, judging by all the wires, there must have been a lot of them.

The visit was late in the afternoon on Friday before Tuesday's election. William flew up to Memphis to come back with the President on Air Force One, along with a number of state officials and campaign leaders. President Carter was to come in for a brief visit in the Mansion, and then go down the front steps for his speech on Capitol Street.

The majestic front columns blended with a lovely, picture book fall evening to provide for a wonderful setting. I remember that the weather was so mild that I was comfortable without a coat. Capitol Street had been closed off for the block in front of the Mansion, and bleachers were set up over the curb to the front fence. The podium for the President was a long carpeted truck bed, with room for several of dignitaries.

After the President had come in with William through the back door, where he was greeted by our family, including my mother, he went to the conference room for a few minutes with some of his staff. From there he walked very briskly through the house. Staff and visiting friends crowded the doorways of the hall, and he stopped and spoke to Mr. and Mrs. Darras and the kitchen staff. Despite all the concerns of the Secret Service, the whole affair moved along on schedule.

The unpublished polls that weekend were showing that President Carter was headed toward a crushing defeat, but I had a very distinct feeling that the President did not know it, or did not believe it. He certainly gave a fine, upbeat speech in front of the Mansion, and I am sure it contributed to his very good showing in Mississippi, which he lost by less than a percentage point.

We at the Mansion had a sense of satisfaction about the affair, and a glow of achievement about the strong support which had been developed in Mississippi despite very heavy odds. Melba and Tommie had prepared a wonderful buffet supper for the family and our special guests after the President had departed. We knew that history had been made for Mississippi that night with the visit of the President, and we were proud to be a part of it.

One small post-election event occurred at the Mansion. Early on the day after, I went outside for my usual morning walk. Hanging on the front gate, just under the Seal of the State of Mississippi, was a pair of men's underwear, torn badly, with a sympathy card pinned to the tear with the words, "Governor, you've torn your drawers in Mississippi."

I didn't think it was very funny, but when I showed the greeting to William he laughed out loud. Later that morning, at a press conference, he held up the underwear and read the card. He and the whole press corps laughed heartily. It helps to have a good sense of humor at the Governor's Mansion.

Reflected in this and nearly everything else William does, I think, is his enjoyment in serving as the Governor of the State of Mississippi. He is giving it the best that he has, and we both consider ourselves fortunate to have participated in the exciting and challenging moments in our days in the Mansion.

Dinner

Gulf Shrimp Elegante

Fleurons

Spinach Salad

Walnut Dressing

Tournedos

Bordelaise Sauce

Squash Supreme

Spring Asparagus

Southern Shortcake

Chenin Blanc
Grenache Rose

The Governor's Mansion
Wednesday, April 1, 1981

Recipes

SOUPS

CREAM OF WATERCRESS SOUP

1 bunch watercress
2 potatoes, thinly sliced and cooked
2 cups chicken broth, or 2 chicken bouillon cubes, 1 cup
cream   and
1 cup water
2 teaspoons parsley
few celery leaves
3 tablespoons flour
2 tablespoons butter
1 teaspoon salt
½ teaspoon white pepper
½ teaspoon monosodium glutamate
1 cup sour cream

Wash and chop watercress (reserve few leaves for garnishing). Place all ingredients into blender and puree. Pour into saucepan and bring to a boil. Reduce heat and simmer 5 minutes. Cool. Chill in refrigerator for several hours before serving. Add 1 cup sour cream just before serving in chilled bowls. Garnish with watercress and thin crisp slices of radish.

A friend from the Delta sent beautiful watercress that was growing in spring water. We loved it and used it several ways. Then, Tommy created this watercress soup for the special Eudora Welty dinner. It was delicious!

MRS. WINTER'S MINT TEA

7 tea bags
12 sprigs of mint
Rind of 3 lemons
8 cups boiling water
Juice of 7 lemons
2 cups sugar
8 cups water

Steep tea, mint and lemon rind in boiling water for 10-12 minutes. Remove tea bags, add juice and sugar. Strain. Add water. Makes 1 gallon.

A friend gave, Deanie Dalrymple me this recipe when we were visiting Monteagle, Tennessee. I loved it and we have used it often. Sometimes we serve it from a punch bowl when we have large crowds. On a hot day it is especially good!

SALADS

SPINACH AND MUSHROOM SALAD

1 pound fresh spinach
6 tablespoons olive oil
2 tablespoons wine vinegar
3 boiled eggs, sliced
½ pound fresh mushrooms, sliced
salt and pepper, to taste
croutons

Wash spinach in several changes of water. Using scissors, trim tough stems and discard. Drain spinach and chill in damp cloth. Tear spinach into bite-sized pieces. Toss with mushrooms and oil and vinegar dressing. Garnish with boiled egg and croutons.

My daughters and I love salads and this is one of our favorites when fresh spinach is available in the early spring.

103

SPINACH SALAD

1 pound fresh spinach, washed well
3 oranges, sectioned (can also use canned mandarin oranges)
1 large avocado
½ cup walnut dressing

Cut away tough stems from spinach and discard, drain well and chill in a damp cloth. Tear into bite-sized pieces. When ready to serve, combine spinach and fruit and season with salt and pepper. Toss with walnut dressing and serve immediately.

This can be changed by omitting the avocado and adding toasted almonds. It's different and we use it often here at the Mansion.

WALNUT DRESSING

6 tablespoons walnut oil (may be obtained at health food store)
2 tablespoons vinegar
salt and pepper

Mix in tightly covered jar and shake well before serving.

TOMMIE DARRAS SHRIMP SALAD

1 pound boiled shrimp
1 cup celery
½ cup sweet relish
3 boiled eggs, chopped
salt and pepper to taste
½ cup mayonnaise

Combine and serve on crisp lettuce leaf.

Shrimp salad is always a treat whether it's served in a pretty tomato or an avocado. This, with a grilled cheese sandwich and a good dessert makes a nice business luncheon for the Governor.

OUR FAVORITE CHICKEN SALAD

2½ cups cooked diced cold chicken
1 cup celery, finely chopped
1 cup sliced white grapes
½ cup chopped toasted almonds
2 tablespoons minced parsley
1 teaspoon salt
1 cup mayonnaise
½ cup whipped cream
   Combine and serve in lettuce cups.
   Tommie often serves this with canteloupe or other fruits. Add warm Peabody muffins and a nice dessert and you have a lovely ladies' luncheon.

MEATS

TOURNEDOS, BORDELAISE SAUCE

Brown sauce:
1 lb. veal bone
¼ carrot, cut up
1 celery rib with leaves
dash thyme
¼ teaspoon crushed peppercorns
1 bay leaf
1 clove garlic (unpeeled)
1 teaspoon salt
2 tablespoons flour
2 cups water
½ cup tomato sauce
Parsley sprigs
   Preheat oven to 450 degrees. Combine bones, onion, carrots, thyme, peppercorn, bay leaf, garlic and salt in roasting pan. Place in oven and bake 45 minutes. Then sprinkle with flour, reduce heat and cook 15 more minutes.

Transfer ingredients to a kettle and add 2 cups water to roaster. Cook over moderate heat, stirring, to dissolve brown particles that cling to bottom and sides. Pour this liquid into kettle and add tomato sauce and parsley. Add additional water if necessary. Bring to rapid boil, reduce heat and simmer 2 hours. Skim fat off often as it rises to surface. Cool and strain.

Bordelaise sauce:
Cook until soft 1 cup chopped onions in ¼ cup butter. Add 2 tablespoons flour and stir until thickened and brown. Gradually add 1 cup brown sauce and cook slowly for 5 minutes. Lastly add 1 tablespoon chopped parsley and taste to adjust seasoning.

Meanwhile, broil tournedos (one per guest) to desired doneness. Place tournedo on plate and blanket with bordelaise or pass sauce.

This is a lot of trouble, but it is delicious and was greatly appreciated and enjoyed by our special guests.

HAWAIIAN CHICKEN

2 tablespoons cornstarch
2 tablespoons water
½ cup vinegar
1 cup sugar
1 cup soy sauce
1 teaspoon ginger
1 teaspoon monosodium glutumate
8 chicken breasts, washed and patted dry
1 can pineapple chunks

Combine first 7 ingredients in saucepan, stir and cook until sauce begins to thicken. Place chicken breasts in baking pan and pour sauce over chicken. Cover and bake for 30 minutes at 400 degrees. Baste frequently. Uncover chicken, reduce heat to 350 degrees and cook for 20 minutes. Add pineapple chunks and cook another 10 minutes.

We have used this recipe often for it can be prepared ahead and kept warm. We served it for a large group when we had supper in the garden and everyone seemed to like it.

CHICKEN IN ROSE SAUCE

4 chicken breasts, split and skinned
4 tablespoons margarine
2 tablespoons flour
¾ cup chicken broth
½ cup rose wine or water
¼ cup thinly sliced green onion
½ cup sliced mushrooms
1 10 ounce package frozen artichoke hearts, cooked according to package directions or 1 14 ounce can artichoke hearts packed in water

Melt 2 tablespoons margarine in baking pan, add chicken breasts and bake at 350 degrees for 30 minutes. Melt remaining margarine in a saucepan, add flour and cook briefly, stirring. Add chicken broth and wine, stirring constantly until sauce is thick and smooth. Remove chicken breasts from oven, turn, and cover each with sliced mushrooms, green onion and artichokes. Pour sauce over all and bake for 30 minutes or until tender.

Yield: 8 servings

We had a luncheon for the officers of the Mississippi Heart Association and we used this chicken recipe from the American Heart Association cookbook. We liked it so much that we have used it often since then.

SEAFOOD

RED SNAPPER AND DARRAS SAUCE

Step one:
Make Darras Sauce
4 tablespoons butter
4 tablespoons flour
2 cups hot milk

Make cream sauce by cooking butter with flour in top part of a double boiler, over low heat, stirring constantly. Add hot milk, gradually, stirring constantly. Place over hot water and cook 10 minutes, stirring frequently. Season to taste with salt and pepper.

1 cup fresh crab meat
½ cup parmesan cheese
1 cup boiled shrimp
dry sherry to taste

Mix the above ingredients and add to cram sauce.

Step two:
6-8 red snapper fillets
Poach in court bouillon
  2 cups water
  1 cup dry white wine
    (or enough to cover fish)
  Juice of 2 lemons and sliced rind
  salt and pepper
  1 tablespoon butter
  1 bay leaf
  1 slice onion
  1 celert rib
  1 carrot, cut into 3 pieces

Simmer all ingredients but fish for 20 minutes. Add fish fillets and cook until done. Remove fish to serving platter and keep warm. Strain court-bouillon and combine with cream sauce. If necessary, thin with heavy cream.

Blanket fish with sauce and sprinkle with fresh chopped parsley or dill.

The Chinese people eat a lot of seafood so we felt this was a safe choice for the dinner for the Chinese Ambassador. It seemed to be greatly appreciated!

SHRIMP REMOULADE

1 cup mayonnaise
1 tablespoon onion juice
dash garlic powder
1 tablespoon fresh tarragon, minced or 1 teaspoon dried
½ teaspoon strong mustard
2 teaspoons anchovy paste
1 tablespoon wine vinegar
4 tablespoons capers
2 tablespoons dry sherry
½ cup chopped parsley

Blend and refrigerate at least overnight before serving on peeled, boiled shrimp over lettuce.

We serve this often as a first course and it is always appreciated. This is an unusually good remoulade sauce.

109

FLOUNDER FILET WITH SEAFOOD SAUCE

This recipe has several steps, but is worth the trouble.
First, make Bechamel sauce:

¼ cup butter
¼ cup flour
½ teaspoon salt
½ teaspoon monosodium glutamate
2 teaspoon paprika
2 cups milk
1 cup cream
2 egg yolks, slightly beaten
1 tablespoon parmesan cheese

Heat butter in saucepan, remove from heat and stir in flour, salt and monosodium glutamate and paprika. Stir til well mixed. Put back on stove, blend in milk and cream. Cook and stir for 1 or 2 more minutes and remove from heat. Stir several tablespoons of the hot mixture into the egg yolks, then add the egg yolks to the mixture. Add parmesan cheese. Continue cooking gently 3-5 minutes while stirring. Take off the heat.

Second, make a seafood sauce:

½ cup chopped parsley
½ cup chopped onion
few celery leaves
1 bay leaf
Dash thyme
½ cup butter
1 cup chopped shrimp
½ cup crabmeat
2 cups Bechamel sauce
½ cup dry white wine

Combine parsley, onion, celery, bay leaf and thyme in butter in a sauce pan. Cook until soft. Add wine and reduce by half. Strain. Add 1 teaspoon salt and ½ teaspoon white pepper, the bechamel sauce, shrimp and

110

crabmeat. The shrimp and crabmeat should be at room temperature.

Meanwhile, place fish fillets in buttered baking pan. Salt and pepper each fillet and dot with butter. Bake until white and flaky. Remove to serving platter and top with seafood sauce.

We love to serve fish but we can't manage it with a large crowd. Flounder is great and comes from our Mississippi Gulf so that makes it even better!

BROILED SHRIMP IN SEASHELLS

2 pounds large shrimp, shelled and deveined
½ cup lemon juice
½ cup olive oil
1 stick butter
2 cloves garlic, crushed and minced
1 tablespoon chopped parsley
¾ teaspoon red pepper (optional)

Wash shrimp, dry, and place in large pan. Mix rest of the ingredients and pour over the shrimp. Let stand in refrigerator overnight. Remove shrimp from marinade and put in heavy skillet. Cook, stirring frequently, until pink. DO NOT OVERCOOK. Fill individual seashells with shrimp and sprinkle with additional chopped parsley.

This makes a very pretty first course and is unusually good.

TROUT ALMONDINE

4 pounds fish fillets
½ cup butter
Salt
Pepper
2 tablespoons lemon juice
chopped parsley
1 package slivered almonds, heated

Arrange fish on long piece of aluminum foil on broiler rack. Place pat of butter on each fillet and broil, allowing 10 minutes per inch of thickness. Turn if the fish is very thick. Just before the fillets are done, sprinkle with lemon juice, salt and pepper and almonds. When done, slide onto serving platter and garnish with chopped parsley.

For a long time I thought this was an especially good recipe for those counting calories. Then I discovered that Tommy had a big pat of butter on each fillet. Since then I've asked him to cut down on the butter and I think it's just as good.

VEGETABLES

SQUASH CASSEROLE

3 cups cooked squash (about 6 medium squash), mashed
½ stick oleo
Salt and pepper to taste
½ to ¾ cup chopped onion (sauteed lightly)
1 cup grated cheddar cheese
½ cup milk
¾ chicken broth
½ cup sour cream
2 eggs, slightly beaten

112

1 cup cracker crumbs (24 crackers, crushed)

Mix all ingredients except cracker crumbs and pour into buttered 2 quart baking dish. Sprinkle crumbs over top and bake 45 minutes at 375 degrees. Serves 8-10.

We have found this to be a Mansion favorite—and especially good when summer squash is available.

HERBED BROILED TOMATOES

4 fresh tomatoes halved
8 pats of butter
salt and pepper to taste
½ teaspoon basil (may also use dill or savory)
½ teaspoon oregano
½ teaspoon parsley
½ cup breadcrumbs

Place halved tomatoes (one slice off bottom so they will stand straight) on baking pan. Combine all ingredients except butter, and cover tomatoes. Place pat of butter in center of each tomato. Bake at 350 degrees until nicely browned. Serves 8.

We use this a lot in the wintertime when the tomatoes are not too flavorful. It adds color to the plate and is very good.

GREEN BEANS ORIENTAL

1 pound fresh green beans
1 cup celery
2 tablespoons cooking oil
½ cup chicken broth
1 teaspoon cornstarch
2 tablespoons water
salt and pepper to taste
3 tablespoons chopped parsley

Cut beans and celery on slant and saute for 1 minute in oil. Add chicken broth. Cover and cook 2 more minutes. Mix cornstarch in water, and add to vegetables. Add salt and pepper and chopped parsley. This should be tender crisp and bright colored.

Variation: add ½ cup water chestnuts, sliced thinly.

Green beans are so often used at banquets where the governor speaks. When we serve green beans here, we want them to be different. We like this recipe.

SQUASH STUFFED WITH CREAMED SPINACH

6 yellow squash
¼ cup chopped onions
1 tablespoon butter
2 cups cooked, chopped fresh spinach, drained thoroughly
3 tablespoons cream sauce
dash nutmeg
salt, pepper to taste
dash Worcestershire sauce

Cut squash lengthwise and scoop out seeds. Sprinkle lightly with salt and pepper and parboil until tender crisp. Place in buttered baking dish.

Make cream sauce with 1 tablespoon butter, 1 tablespoon flour and a little milk. Saute onions in butter until tender, combine with spinach, cream sauce and seasonings. Fill squash cavity, bake at 350 degrees until hot.

I am not a big spinach eater, but I like this. It's different to look at and to eat.

GREEN BEAN CASSEROLE

1 can green beans, drained
1 can cream of mushroom soup
salt and pepper to taste
1 can fried onion rings
½ cup grated cheese
   Combine all ingredients, mix well. Bake at 350 degrees until bubbly.
   This is a very easy recipe—great for an inexperienced cook or an experienced cook in a hurry!

CHEESE GRITS

1 cup grits
1 teaspoon garlic salt
8 ounces grated cheese
1 stick butter
2 egg yolks, beaten and put in measuring cup and fill to one cup with milk
2 egg whites
   Cook grits. Add cheese, butter and salt. Add egg yolks and milk mixture. Carefully fold in stiffly beaten egg whites. Pour into greased casserole. Bake at 300 degrees for 35 minutes.
   We serve this for breakfast often when we have special guests. It's great, too, for a brunch before a football game.

BREADS

HOT CRAB CANAPES

¼ cup butter
2 tablespoons flour
1 cup cream
salt and pepper
4 ounces swiss cheese, grated
¼ cup sherry
1 pound fresh crabmeat

Melt butter, add flour then cream to make heavy cream sauce. Add grated cheese, sherry and picked crabmeat. Season with salt and pepper. Spoon onto toast rounds and run under broiler until bubbly. May also serve from chafing dish.

We served these at the tea for "Miss Lillian" Carter. It is also nice on toast for luncheon.

CHEESE WAFERS

1 pound sharp cheese
1 stick butter
2 cups flour
1 teaspoon salt
dash tabasco, or pinch of red pepper

Grate cheese. Melt butter and pour over cheese. Mix other ingredients. Press from cookie press, or roll in waxed paper, chill and slice thinly. Bake at 400 degrees for 8-10 minutes.

We frequently serve these wafers at the Mansion. The Chinese Delegation particularly enjoyed them.

MINNIE'S HOMEMADE CINNAMON PINWHEELS

2½ cups flour
1 heating tablespoon sugar
2 teaspoons baking powder
½ cup shortening
1 teaspoon salt
1 pkg. dry yeast dissolved in ¼ cup warm water
¾ cup buttermilk

Combine dry ingredients. Cut in shortening until consistency of corn meal. Combine milk and yeast mixture and add to flour and shortening. Mix well together, kneading like biscuit dough. Roll out ¼ inch thick. Sprinkle with mixture of:

1 cup brown sugar
1 tablespoon cinnamon
½ cup raisins
2 tablespoons chopped nuts
½ stick melted butter

Roll for jelly roll and slice. Bake at 400 degrees until golden brown.

While baking, make frosting:

½ box confectioners sugar
½ teaspoon vanilla
¼ stick butter, melted
Enough milk to make mixture thin enough to spread

Combine and spread on warm rolls.

The Governor has the elected state officials for breakfast each month. Minnie's pinwheels seem to be a favorite with this group.

BRAN MUFFINS

1 pound box bran cereal
5 cups flour
5 teaspoons soda
1 teaspoon salt
4 eggs beaten
3 cups sugar
1 quart buttermilk
1 cup salad oil

Mix dry ingredients. Gradually add eggs, oil and milk. Bake in hot oven (400 degrees) about 12-15 minutes. Unused portion may be stored in refrigerator for 6 weeks and used as needed.

These are delicious—especially good for breakfast. They can be made in small muffin tins and used for brunch. Dates and nuts may be added, too.

HOT CHEESE PUFFS

8 ounces sharp cheddar cheese, grated very fine (Kraft yellow foil wrapper)
½ cup mayonnaise
1 egg
½ teaspoon cayenne pepper (or to taste)
1 loaf thinly sliced bread

Grate cheese, set aside to soften. Beat egg with electric mixer; add mayonnaise and continue beating. Stir the egg mixture into the grated cheese. Cut small rounds from bread (the size of a quarter). Spread cheese mixture on rounds and place on ungreased cookie sheet. Bake at 375 degrees until cheese bubbles and begins to brown—about 10-12 minutes. You can broil until cheese bubbles and begins to brown if you are in a hurry. These freeze nicely before baking.

This recipe was given to me by Mrs. Eddy Dalton, wife of the former Governor of Virginia. I first tasted this when Eddy had the Governors' wives for coffee during the Southern Governors' Association meeting in Williamsburg. We've used it often here at the Mansion and like it very much.

HOTEL PEABODY VANILLA MUFFINS

2 cups sugar
4 eggs
4 cups flour
2 cups milk
1 tablespoon baking powder
1 tablespoon vanilla
1 stick melted butter

Beat sugar and eggs together, add flour, milk and baking powder, stir well. Add melted butter and vanilla. Bake in warmed muffin pans, well greased. Makes 36.

These are a special treat when we have light luncheons of fruit salad. The Peabody Hotel is a landmark in Memphis, Tennessee.

SPANIKOPITA

2 pounds fresh spinach, washed, drained & chopped
1 bunch green onions finely chopped
¼ cup minced parsley
¼ teaspoon dill
1 cup crumbled feta cheese
6 eggs, beaten
½ pound melted butter
½ pound phyllo

Saute onions in olive oil until soft. Add spinach and parsley and cook until wilted. Combine all ingredients and salt lightly.

Layer 6 sheets phyllo, buttering each sheet, in 9 × 13 × 2 pan. Spread with spinach mixture. Then top with 6 additional layers of phyllo, buttering each one.

Bake at 350 degrees for 40 minutes. Cool and cut into squares.

This is another traditional Greek dish that Tommie Darras serves and all of us enjoy. It's very good for a buffet.

TOASTED BREAD FINGERS

Trim bread and cut into finger slices. Roll in melted butter, then roll in sesame seeds. Toast in very slow oven about 200 degrees until completely crisp and nicely browned. May serve warm or room temperature. These will keep indefinitely in tightly covered tin.

We sometimes serve these bread fingers instead of crackers with salad. It's a nice change.

SPINACH PINWHEELS

2 pounds fresh spinach
1 onion, minced
3 tablespoons olive oil
½ cup butter
6 eggs, beaten
1 cup finely crumbled feta cheese
½ cup fresh dill, chopped, or 1 tablespoon dried dill
½ cup finely chopped parsley
salt, pepper to taste
½ pound phyllo pastry
melted butter

Wash spinach in several changes of water. Dry it and chop finely. Cook in oil until wilted. Drain. Saute onion in butter until soft. Mix onion, eggs, feta cheese, dill and parsley. Add salt and pepper.

Place 6 sheets of phyllo pastry on waxed paper, brushing each with melted butter. Spread evenly with spinach mixture. Roll as for jelly roll and hold together with waxed paper. Chill. Slice thinly and bake until golden brown at 400 degrees. This makes three rolls.

These pinwheels are a little different, and very good. We used them for the Leontyne Price dinner.

HAM AND ASPARAGUS ROLLS

Thin-sliced bread (light or dark)
Asparagus spears
Home-made mayonnaise
Thin-sliced ham

Flatten each slice of bread with rolling pin. Spread bread with mayonnaise and top with thinly-sliced ham. Place an asparagus spear on each slice. Roll like a jelly roll, secure with tooth pick. Place cut side down in pan, toast and serve warm.

Variation: Use any herbed butter rather than mayonnaise.

We have served these with a salad at a ladies luncheon or at a coffee or buffet.

DESSERTS

APPLE CAKE

1 cup oil
2 cups sugar
3 eggs, well beaten
2½ cups flour
1 teaspoon salt
1 teaspoon soda
2 teaspoons baking powder
2 teaspoons cinnamon
1 teaspoon nutmeg
1 teaspoon vanilla
3 cups chopped apples
1 cup pecans

Combine oil and sugar. Add eggs. Mix until creamy. Gradually add 2¼ cup flour (reserve rest for fruit) salt, baking powder, soda, and spices. Fold in vanilla. Add fruit and nuts that have been mixed with remaining ¼ cup flour.

Bake in a greased and floured pan 13 × 9 × 2 at 300 degrees for 1 hour. Frost with caramel icing or cream cheese icing when cool.

CREAM CHEESE ICING

1 (1 pound) box confectioner's sugar
1 (8 ounce) package cream cheese
½ cup margarine
2 teaspoons vanilla
1 cup chopped pecans

Have all ingredients at room temperature. In a large bowl with mixer at low speed beat sugar, cream cheese and margarine until smooth. Add vanilla; then stir in pecans.

This apple cake is one I've made often at home and we like it very much. It's really moist and good.

MISSISSIPPI MUD CAKE

1 cup butter
½ cup cocoa
2 cups sugar
4 eggs, slightly beaten
1½ cups chopped pecans
1½ cups flour
salt
vanilla
Miniature marshmallows
chocolate frosting

Melt butter and cocoa together. Remove from heat. Stir in sugar and beaten eggs, mix well. Add flour, pinch of salt and nuts and 1 teaspoon vanilla. Mix well. Spoon batter into greased and floured 13 × 9 × 2 pan and bake at 350 degrees for 35 to 45 minutes. Sprinkle marshmallows on top of hot cake. Cover with chocolate frosting.

CHOCOLATE FROSTING

1 box powdered sugar
½ cup milk
⅓ cup cocoa
½ stick butter

Combine sugar, milk, cocoa and butter and mix until smooth. Spread on hot cake. We often receive requests for recipes and I've sent this one all over the country.

FUDGE CAKE

2 sticks butter
4 eggs
4 squares bitter chocolate, melted
1⅓ cups flour
2 cups sugar
1 cup pecans, chopped
1 teaspoon vanilla
pinch of salt

Cream butter and sugar, add eggs one at a time. Add melted chocolate. Mix flour, salt and nuts. Add to chocolate mixture. Add vanilla. Pour into greased 13 × 9 × 2 pan. Bake at 275 degrees for 45 minutes. Cool, then cut into squares.

This is a recipe I've used at home for years. The girls especially like it. I've sent this to them when they were away in school and I understand it never lasts long. I usually frost this cake with the same chocolate frosting used on the Mississippi Mud cake.

COCONUT CHESS PIE

1 cup sugar
1 stick butter, room temperature
2 teaspoons flour
4 eggs, slightly beaten
1 cup milk
1 cup grated coconut
2 teaspoons vanilla
1 prepared pie pastry

Cream together sugar, butter and flour. Add eggs and mix well. Add milk, coconut and vanilla. Pour into un-baked pie pastry. Bake at 400 degrees for 10 minutes, then reduce temperature to 325 degrees for 15 minutes or until tooth pick comes out clean when inserted in center. Serve warm.

PECAN PIE

½ cup sugar
1 cup white karo
3 eggs, well beaten
1 cup pecans
½ stick butter
1 teaspoon vanilla

Cream butter and sugar, add eggs and mix thoroughly. Add karo and vanilla. Pour into unbaked pastry shell and bake at 450 degrees for 10 minutes, then reduce to 350 degrees for 30 minutes or until firm. When the oven heat is lowered, set a pan of water directly over the pie. It will not brown any more.

William is very partial to this pie. It is grand and the cooks in the kitchen spoil him with it!

MRS. WINTER'S ORANGE CHARLOTTE

1 package orange-flavored gelatin
1 package lemon-flavored gelatin
2 cups orange juice, boiling hot
1 cup boiling water
⅓ cup sugar
½ pint cream
Sweetened whipped cream
Coconut
Mint leaves

To boiling orange juice and water, add gelatin and sugar. Let stand until cool. Let congeal until thick. When thick, whip and then fold in ½ pint cream, whipped. Pour into large greased ring mold. Refrigerate until firm. When ready to serve, unmold and ice with sweetened whipped cream. Sprinkle with coconut and garnish with mint leaves. Serve on a silver tray.

This is a pretty dessert. I've used it many times at home. It's easy to make and is a Winter favorite. The recipe was given to me by my sister, Virginia Phillips, years ago. Many of my favorite recipes have come from her. She is a grand cook!

ENGLISH TRIFLE

3 cups milk
1½ cups sugar
2 tablespoons flour
5 egg yolks
1 teaspoon vanilla

1 banana, sliced
½ cup fresh of frozen raspberries
½ cup fresh or frozen peaches
½ cup fresh or frozen strawberries
Lady fingers

Heat milk in top of double boiler. Meanwhile, mix sugar and flour. Add egg yolks and blend well. Add slowly to milk, stirring with a wire whisk. Return to double boiler and cook over hot, not boiling water, stirring constantly until it coats a silver spoon Cool quickly by placing pan in cold water. Strain and add vanilla.

In a cutglass bowl, alternate layers of custard and lady fingers that have been soaked in sherry. Begin and end with custard layer. Garnish with swirls of sweetened whipped cream, fresh strawberries and angelica.

This makes a beautiful dessert and is really lovely for a special occasion.

CHERRIES JUBILEE

2 cans pitted Bing cherries
1 teaspoon nutmeg
2/3 cup sugar
1 teaspoon arrowroot
1/4 teaspoon almond extract

Combine above ingredients in serving dish, add 1/2 cup brandy. Flame and serve over pound cake topped with vanilla ice cream.

This makes a spectacular dessert. We served it for the dinners we had in 1980 for the members of the Legislature and their wives.

PEACH MELBA

In individual dessert compotes place a lady finger or square of sponge cake on bottom. Top with vanilla ice cream then a liberal layer of fresh peaches. Crown with fresh raspberry melba sauce and whipped cream.

RASPBERRY MELBA SAUCE

1½ teaspoons cornstarch
1 tablespoon raspberry juice
1 package frozen raspberries (or fresh if available)
1½ cup currant jelly

Blend cornstarch with 1 tablespoon raspberry juice from package of raspberries. Heat thawed raspberries with currant jelly. Stir in cornstarch mixture. Cook, stirring constantly, until thick and clear. Cool.

We love to serve this. It's easy and makes a beautiful dessert. Tablecloths beware—the raspberry stain is hard to remove! We served this first for the Eudora Welty dinner.

127

CREAMY CARAMEL ICING

2½ cups sugar
1 slightly beaten egg
1 stick butter
¾ cup milk
1 teaspoon vanilla

Melt ½ cup of sugar in iron skillet slowly, until brown and runny. Mix egg, butter, remaining sugar, and milk in a saucepan and cook over a low flame until butter melts. Turn the heat up to medium and add the browned sugar. Cook until it reaches the soft ball stage or until mixture leaves sides of pan. This takes about 10 minutes. Remove from fire, let cool slightly and add vanilla. Beat until right consistency to spread. If it gets too thick, add a little cream. This will ice a two-layer cake.

This is a little tricky to do but it's well worth the effort. I think this is the all-time favorite at my house and another of my sister's recipes.

SOUTHERN STRAWBERRY SHORTCAKE

Southern Shortcake
½ cup butter
⅔ cup light cream
1 egg
½ teaspoon salt
3 teaspoons baking powder
2 tablespoons sugar
2 cups flour

Sift dry ingredients together, cut in butter. Combine egg and cream and mix thoroughly. Add all at once to dry mixture, stirring just enough to moisten. Roll to one-half inch thickness. Cut with 2½ inch cutter. Bake at 450 degrees for 15 minutes. Split each shortcake and top with fresh, sweetened strawberries. Just before serving pour sauce over each serving and top with whipped cream.

Sauce
1 egg, well beaten
1 cup sugar
½ cup water
   Stir together. Cook, stirring constantly over low heat.
Serve warm over shortcakes.
   *This was my mother's recipe. Strawberry shortcake at home was
never complete without this sauce. It's worth the extra calories!*

SOUR CREAM COFFEE CAKE
1½ cup sifted flour
¼ teaspoon salt
1 teaspoon baking powder
1 teaspoon soda
1 cup sugar
¾ cup shortening
2 eggs
1 cup sour cream
1 teaspoon vanilla

TOPPING
¾ cup sugar
1 teaspoon cinnamon
¼ cup pecans, chopped
   Sift together flour, salt, baking powder and soda. Blend
1 cup sugar with shortening; and eggs. Add sour cream
and vanilla to shortening mixture; add sifted dry ingredients. Beat until smooth. Spread half of batter in greased
tube pan, sprinkle with topping; spread rest of batter and
cover top with remaining topping. Bake 45 minutes in 325
degree oven. Serves 8-10.
   *This is a recipe I loved to make at home. It's really good and someone
always asks for the recipe. It keeps well unless your family loves it like
mine does!*

MINT ICE CREAM

1½ cup sugar
1½ cup water
1 cup fresh mint leaves, washed
1 #2 can crushed pineapple
4 tablespoons lemon juice (or may use 8 tablespoons of orange juice)
2 cups milk
2 cups cream, lightly whipped
Green food coloring, if desired.

Cook and stir sugar and water until it boils. Cook to soft boil and add mint leaves. Cook 15 minutes longer. Remove from heat. Strain and let cool. Add remaining ingredients except cream. Partially freeze, then stir in whipped cream. Freeze until firm. Makes 2 quarts.

This is really my favorite ice cream. I love the fresh mint flavor and I like the idea that the mint has come from our garden. Guests seem to like this too.

COOKIES

STAR COOKIES

3 ounces cream cheese
1 cup butter
1 cup sugar
1 egg yolk
1 teaspoon vanilla
2½ cup flour

Cream butter and cheese, add egg yolk and sugar. Mix well. Add flour, then vanilla. Using the star tube, press through pastry bag. Bake for 8 minutes in a 375 degree oven. When cool, decorate with pastel icing, if desired.

ICING FOR COOKIES

2 tablespoons butter, melted
2 cups sifted confectioners sugar
4 tablespoons milk
1 teaspoon vanilla

In medium bowl, with electric mixer on medium speed, beat until smooth. Can be tinted with food coloring if desired. Spread on cookies when cooled.

Minnie and Lorene make these in the Mansion kitchen constantly. We try not to let the cookie tins get empty!

BAKLAVA

1 lb. blanched almonds, finely chopped
1 cup sugar
1 tablespoon cinnamon
1 lb. phyllo (available at frozen food counter)
2 cups melted butter
Syrup (below)

Combine almonds, sugar and cinnamon. Place 6 sheets phyllo in 9 × 13 × 2 pan, brushing each sheet with melted butter. Sprinkle generously with nut mixture. Continue process using only 3 sheets phyllo until all nut mixture is used. Place 6 more phyllo sheets on top, buttering each one. Cut baklava into diamond-shaped pieces. Heat remaining butter and pour over baklava.

Place pan of water on lowest shelf of 300 degree oven and bake baklava for 3 hours. Remove from oven and pour cool syrup over.

Syrup
1 cup sugar
½ cup honey
2 cups water
Juice of 1 lemon

Boil for 20 minutes and cool.

Tommie is from Greece and he loves to bake and eat this. It's really great.

PECAN TASSIES

3 ounces cream cheese, softened
1 stick butter
1 cup flour

Mix above ingredients until smooth. Chill. Shape and fit into miniature muffin tins.

¾ cup brown sugar
1 tablespoon melted butter
1 teaspoon vanilla
½ cup pecans, chopped

Combine above ingredients, spoon into each tassie shell. Bake at 350 degrees for 25 minutes. Makes about 3 dozen.

This is a miniature southern pecan pie. It's good as a pick-up sweet for a tea or coffee. It's a lot of trouble but worth it.

CHESS SQUARES

1 cup butter
1 box butter cake mix
1 egg

Combine and put in pan 9 × 13. Bake 15 minutes at 350 degrees. Remove from oven and top with:

3 eggs
1 box powdered sugar
1 8 ounce cream cheese

Beat together and pour over crust. Bake at 325 degrees for 35 minutes. Cut into squares.

This is a recipe I used at home. It's very simple, but good.

MISSISSIPPI COOKIES

2 cups flour
1 teaspoon baking powder
½ teaspoon salt
½ cup shortening
1 cup sugar
1 egg
4 tablespoons milk
½ teaspoon vanilla

Cream shortening and sugar, stir in egg. Combine vanilla and milk, add alternately with sifted dry ingredients. Chill dough overnight. Preheat oven to 400 degrees. Roll dough as thinly as possible and cut with cookie cutter. Sprinkle with sugar. Bake on greased cookie sheet about 8 minutes or until nicely browned.

At the Mansion, we like to use a cookie cutter in the shape of the state of Mississippi. We first used these at the Inaugural Tea and they were truly distinctive.

MINNIE MILLER'S CHOCOLATE CHIP COOKIES

1 cup butter
1 cup brown sugar, packed
¾ cup white sugar
2 eggs
2¼ cups sifted flour
1 teaspoon soda
½ teaspoon salt
2 teaspoons vanilla extract
1 (12 ounce) package chocolate morsels
1 cup chopped pecans

Cream butter and sugars. Add vanilla. Lightly beat eggs. Mix dry ingredients. Add alternately with eggs. Add pecans. Mix in chocolate morsels. Drop by teaspoonfuls onto greased baking sheet. Bake at 375 degrees for 10-12 minutes. Makes 6 dozen.

My girls love these cookies. They always expect to find them in tins on the kitchen shelf when they come home. We try to keep them on hand, but they go in a hurry!

QUICK LEMON CRISPS

¾ cup shortening
1 cup sugar
2 (3¾ oz.) pkg. lemon instant pudding mix
¼ teaspoon lemon flavoring
3 eggs
2 cups sifted all-purpose flour
¼ teaspoon soda

Cream shortening, sugar and pudding mix until light and fluffy. Add lemon flavoring. Add eggs and beat well. Add flour and soda to mixture and mix well. Mixture will be stiff. Drop from teaspoon about 2½ inches apart on greased cookie sheet. Bake at 350 degrees for 8 to 10 minutes. Yield: About 6 dozen cookies.

We're always looking for new cookie recipes. We have quite a few teas so we need to make cookies in large quantities.

LEMON SQUARES

1½ cup butter
2 cups flour
½ cup powdered sugar
4 eggs, beaten
Juice of 2 lemons and grated rind
2 cups sugar
1 teaspoon baking powder
4 tablespoons flour

Cut butter into flour and powdered sugar. Pat into 9 X 13 pan. Bake at 350 degrees for 15 minutes.

Mix eggs and lemon juice. Combine remaining ingredients and add to egg mixture. Pour over pastry. Return to oven and bake at 350 degrees for 25 minutes.

While warm, sprinkle with powdered sugar.

Cool and cut into squares.

These lemon squares can be made a day or two ahead and kept in a cookie tin. They are very good to serve at a tea or coffee—an easy pickup dessert.

MINIATURE CHEESE CAKES

Butter
10 Graham crackers, crushed
1 (8 ounce) package cream cheese, softened
¾ cup sugar
3 eggs separated
1 cup sour cream
3 tablespoons sugar
1 teaspoon vanilla

Butter sides and bottoms of all 48 sections in 4 miniature muffin tins. Sprinkle with Graham cracker crumbs and shake to coat. Mix well the cream cheese and sugar, add egg yolks, one at a time, beating well. Fold in stiffly beaten egg whites. Spoon into miniature muffin tins and bake at 350 degrees for 15 minutes. While cooling, combine sour cream, sugar, and vanilla. Top each cake with a spoon of sour cream and bake 5 minutes more. Let cool in pan. Garnish with a fresh strawberry. Makes 48.

This is a nice pick-up dessert for a tea or coffee. If you like cheese cake, you'll love this.

JACK-O-LANTERN COOKIES

Use same recipe as for Mississippi cookies. Cut these out with a jack-o-lantern cutter. When cookies are cooled, decorate them with orange and chocolate frosting.

We don't have too many trick-or-treaters, since the Governor's Mansion is in downtown Jackson, but everybody here knows when Hallowe'en comes because of the cookies and the jack-o-lantern on the front porch.